FOR ORGANS, PIANOS & ELECTRONIC KEYBOARDS

E-Z PLAY TODAY

171

2ND EDITION

The Best of
ELTON JOHN

ISBN 978-0-7935-9138-1

HAL•LEONARD®
CORPORATION
7777 W. BLUEMOUND RD. P.O. BOX 13819 MILWAUKEE, WI 53213

E-Z PLAY ® TODAY Music Notation © 1975 by HAL LEONARD CORPORATION

E-Z PLAY and EASY ELECTRONIC KEYBOARD MUSIC are registered trademarks of HAL LEONARD CORPORATION.

Visit Hal Leonard Online at
www.halleonard.com

The Best of
ELTON JOHN

CONTENTS

Bennie and the Jets

Registration 4
Rhythm: Rock or 8 Beat

Words and Music by Elton John
and Bernie Taupin

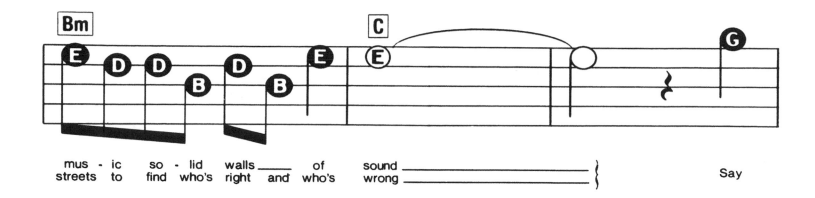

mus - ic so - lid walls _____ of sound _____ } Say
streets to find who's right and who's wrong _____

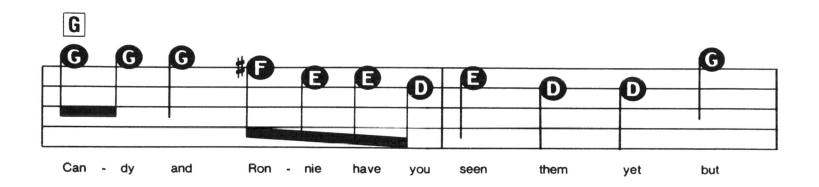

Can - dy and Ron - nie have you seen them yet but

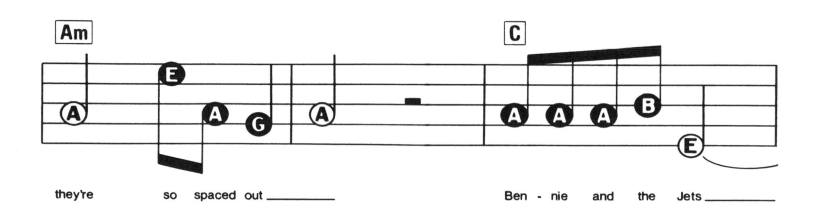

they're so spaced out _____ Ben - nie and the Jets _____

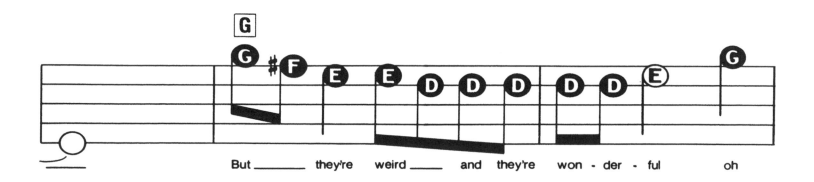

But _____ they're weird _____ and they're won - der - ful oh

6

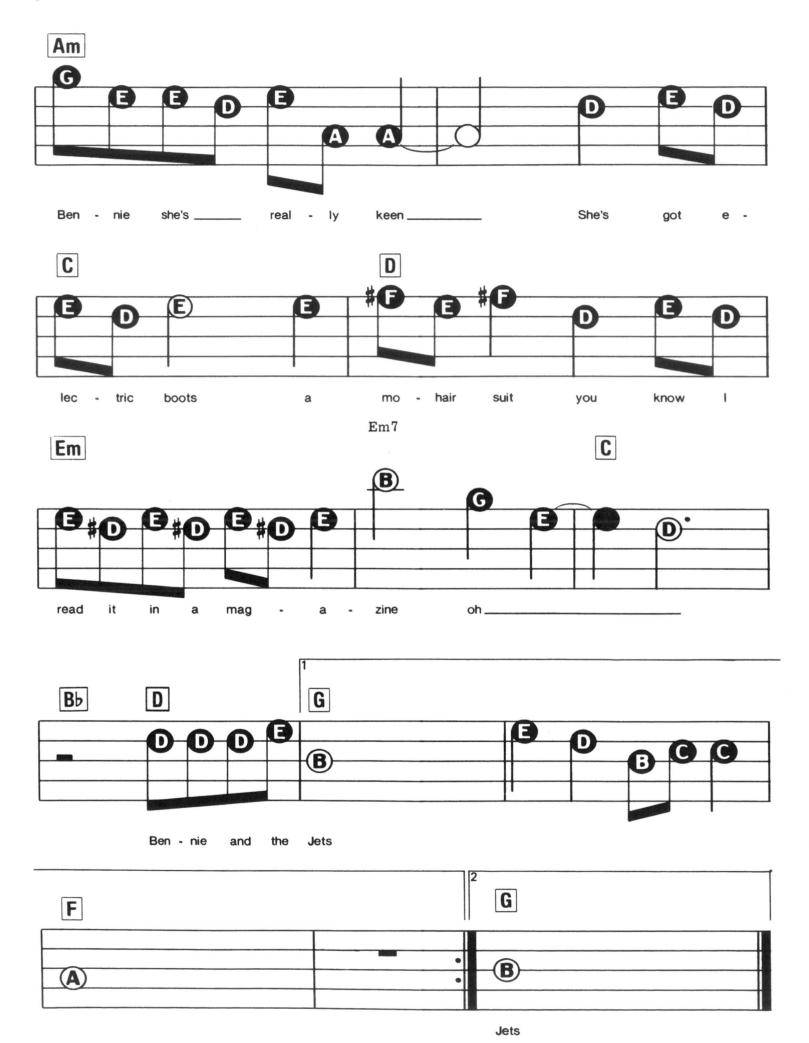

Can You Feel the Love Tonight
from Walt Disney Pictures' THE LION KING

Registration 2
Rhythm: Rock or 8 Beat

Music by Elton John
Lyrics by Tim Rice

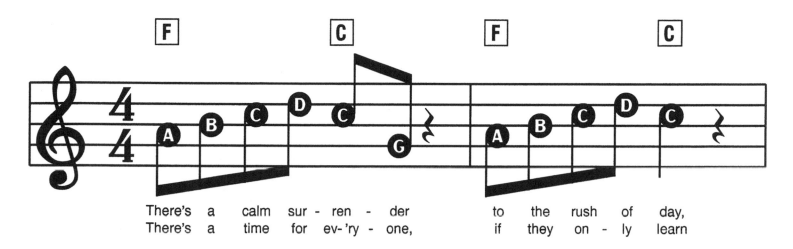

There's a calm sur - ren - der to the rush of day,
There's a time for ev-'ry - one, if they on - ly learn

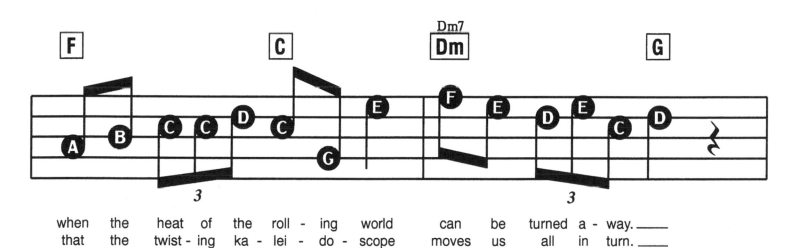

when the heat of the roll - ing world can be turned a - way. ____
that the twist - ing ka - lei - do - scope moves us all in turn. ____

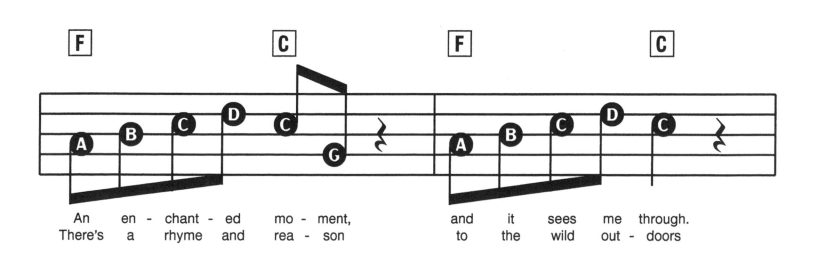

An en - chant - ed mo - ment, and it sees me through.
There's a rhyme and rea - son to the wild out - doors

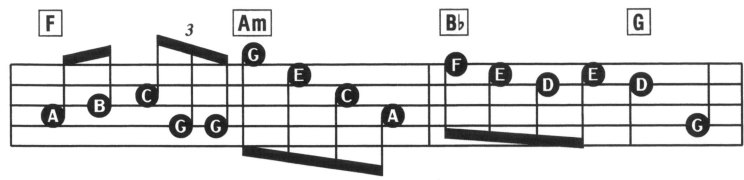

It's e - nough for this rest - less war - rior just to be with you.
when the heart of this star - crossed voy - ag - er beats in time with yours. } And

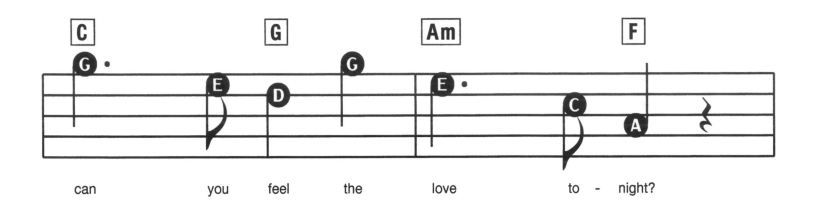

can you feel the love to - night?

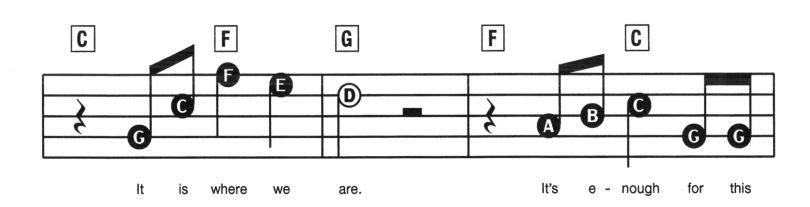

It is where we are. It's e - nough for this

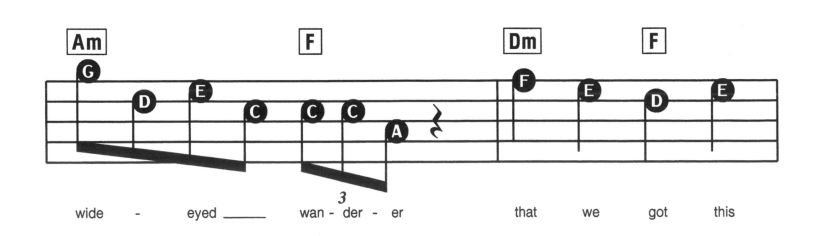

wide - eyed _____ wan - der - er that we got this

Border Song

Registration 6
Rhythm: Swing or Pops

Words and Music by Elton John
and Bernie Taupin

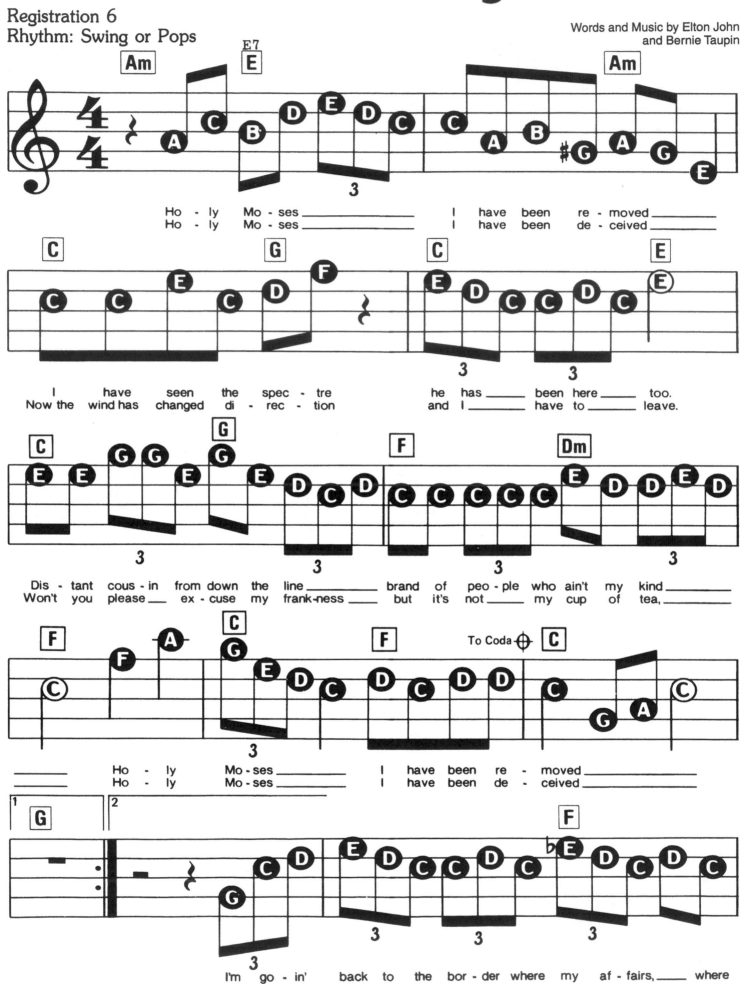

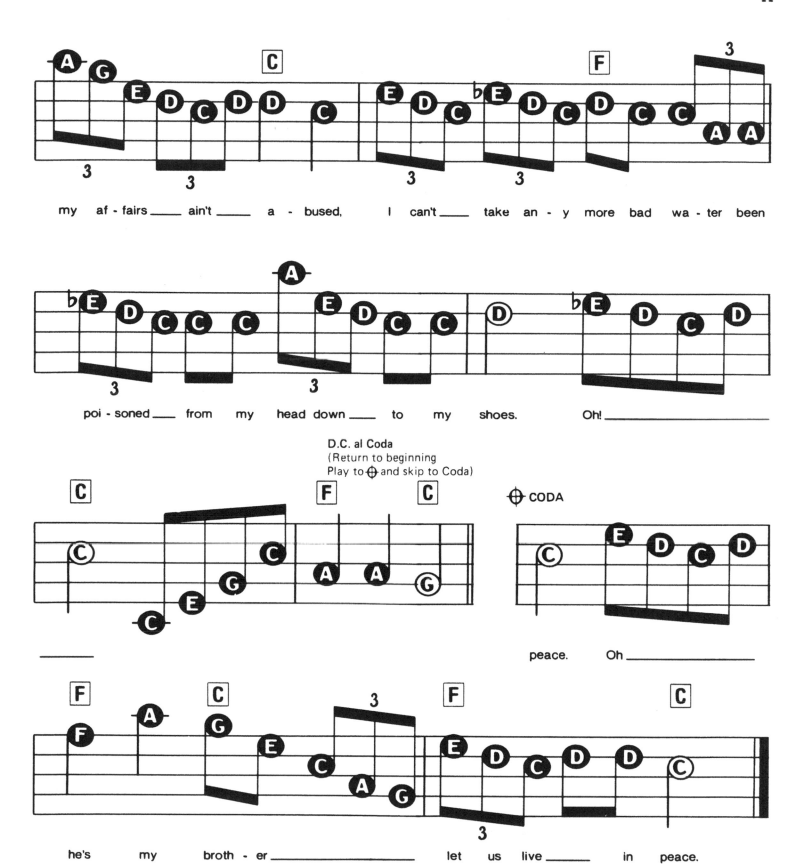

my af - fairs ___ ain't ___ a - bused, I can't ___ take an - y more bad wa - ter been

poi - soned ___ from my head down ___ to my shoes. Oh! _____

D.C. al Coda
(Return to beginning
Play to ⊕ and skip to Coda)

⊕ CODA

___ peace. Oh _____

he's my broth - er _____ let us live ___ in peace.

3. Holy Moses Let us live in peace,
   Let us strive to find a way
   to make all hatred ceace.
   There's a man over there,
   What's his color I don't care,
   He's my brother, Let us live in peace.
   Oh he's my brother let us live in peace.

Candle in the Wind

Registration 8
Rhythm: Rock or 8 Beat

Words and Music by Elton John
and Bernie Taupin

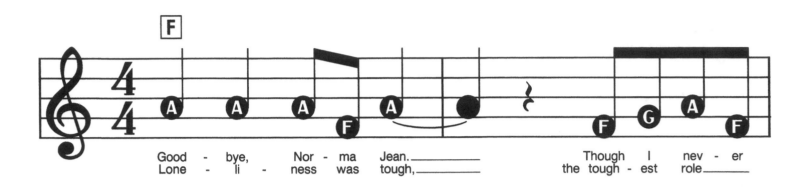

Good - bye, Nor - ma Jean._____ Though I nev - er
Lone - li - ness was tough,_____ the tough - est role

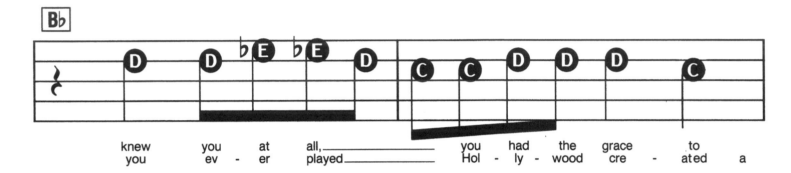

knew you at all,_____ you had the grace to
you ev - er played_____ Hol - ly - wood cre - at ed a

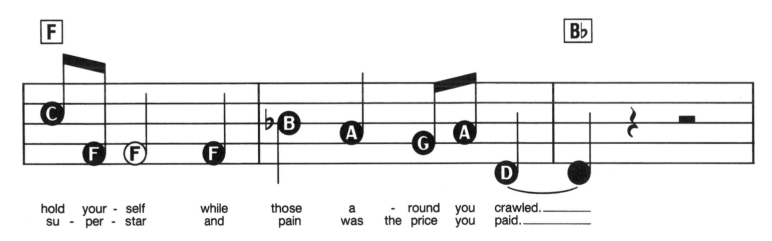

hold your - self while those a - round you crawled._____
su - per - star and pain was the price you paid._____

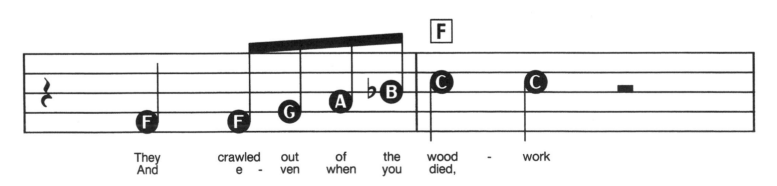

They crawled out of the wood - work
And e - ven when you died,

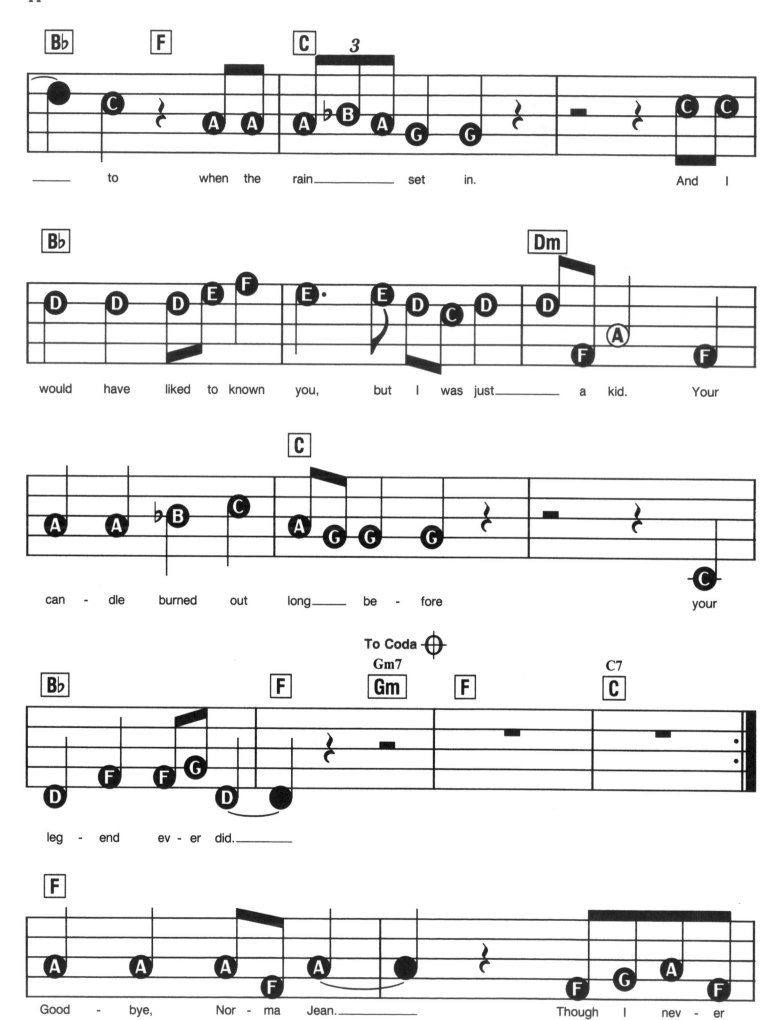

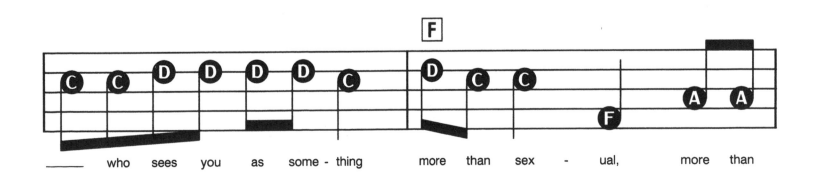

D.S. al Coda
(Return to ％
Play to ⊕ and
skip to Coda)

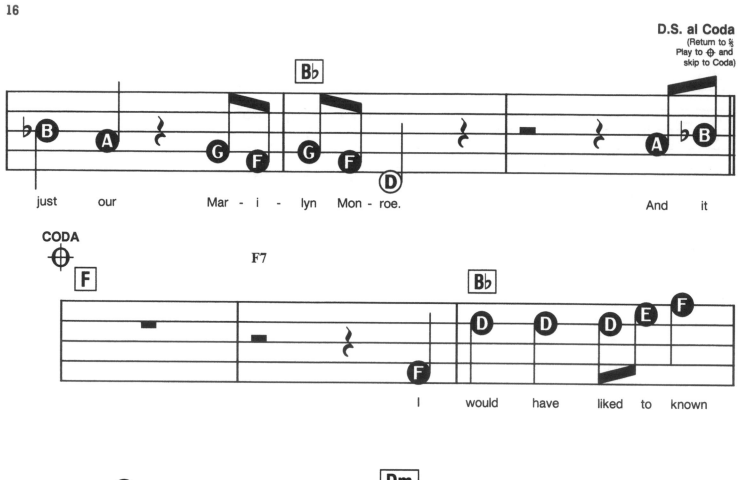

just   our   Mar - i - lyn Mon - roe.   And it

CODA

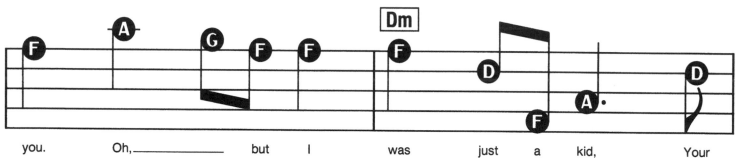

I   would have liked to known

you.   Oh,_____ but   I   was   just   a   kid,   Your

can - dle burned out   long_____ be - fore_____

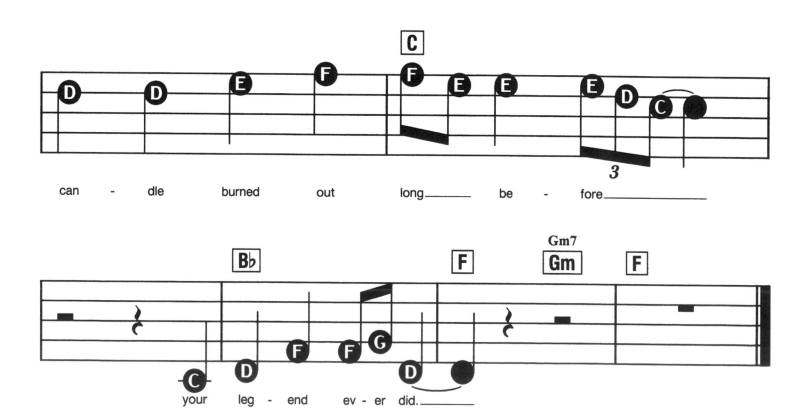

your   leg - end ev - er did._____

Crocodile Rock

Registration 5
Rhythm: Rock

Words and Music by Elton John
and Bernie Taupin

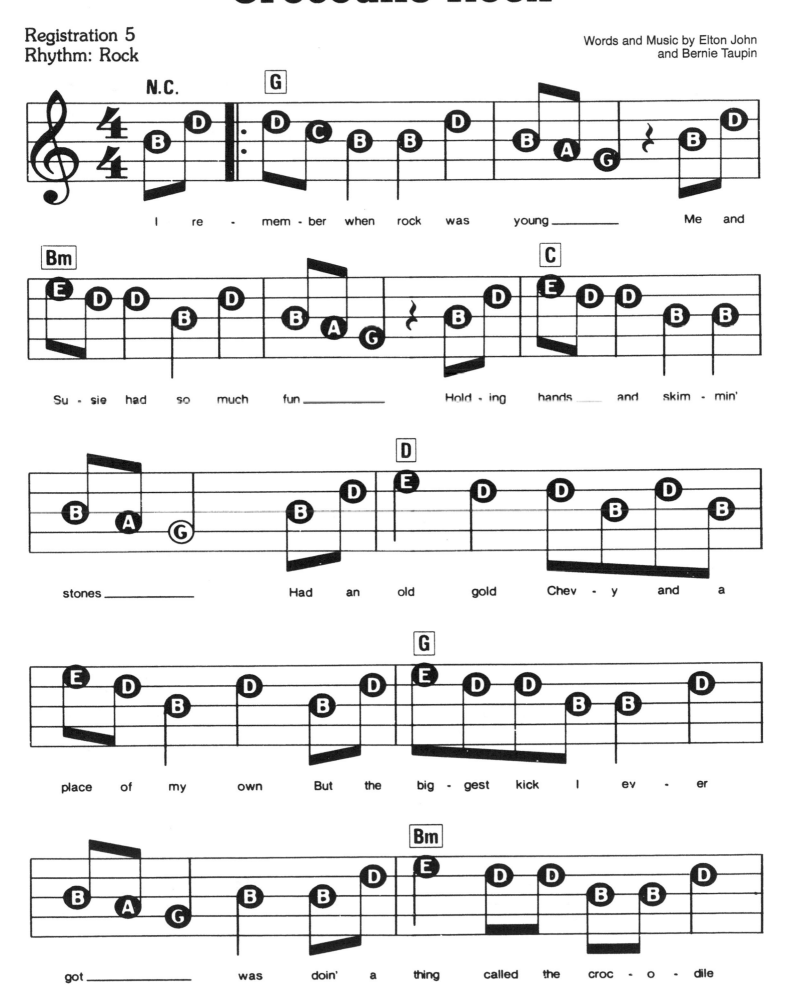

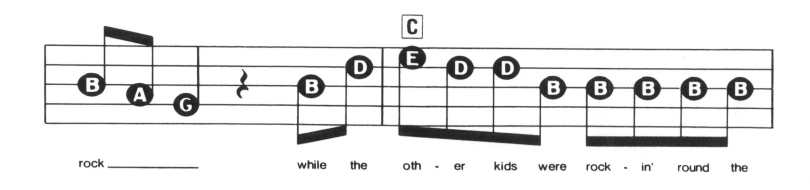

rock _____ while the oth - er kids were rock - in' round the

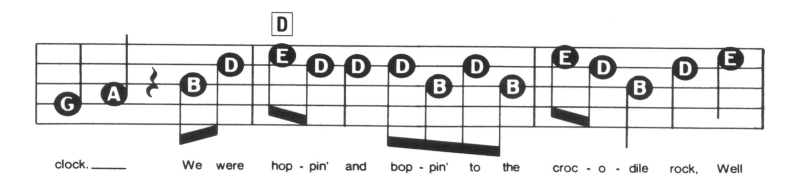

clock. ____ We were hop - pin' and bop - pin' to the croc - o - dile rock, Well

CHORUS

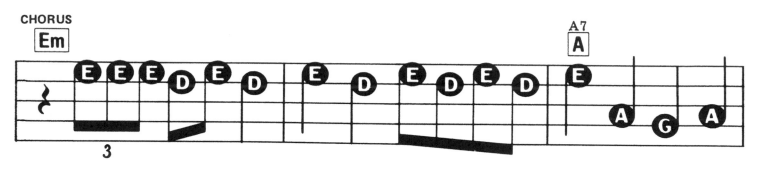

croc - o - dile rock - in' is some - thing shock - in' when your feet just can't keep

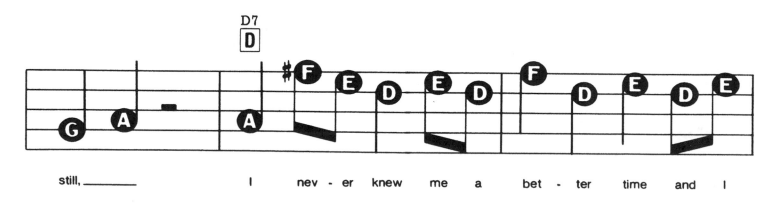

still, _____ I nev - er knew me a bet - ter time and I

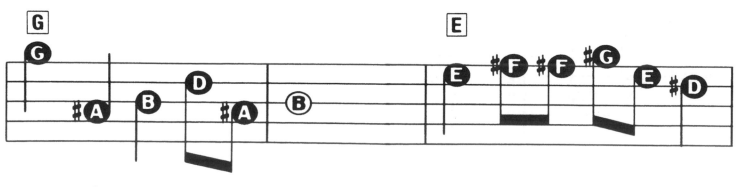

guess I nev - er _____ will. Oh Lawd - y ma - ma those

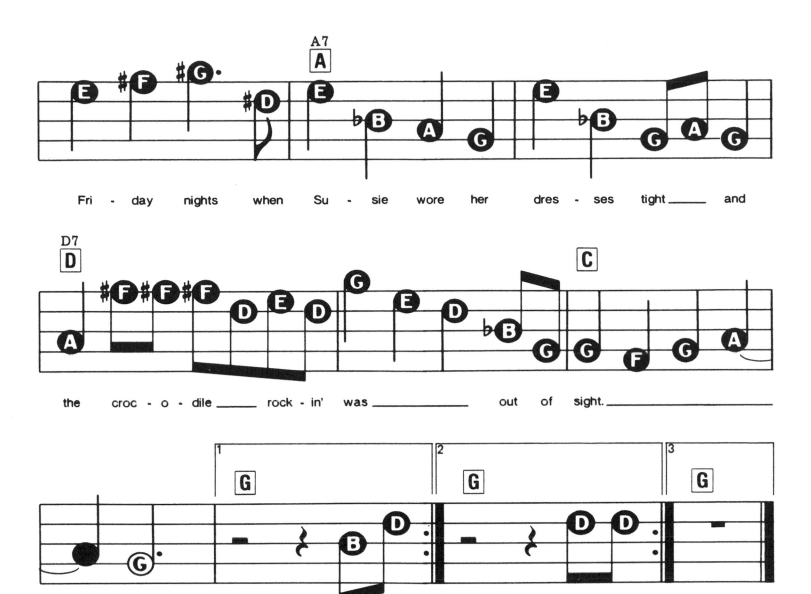

Fri - day nights when Su - sie wore her dres - ses tight____ and

the croc - o - dile ____ rock - in' was _____ out of sight._____

_____ But the I re -

Additional Lyrics

2. (But the) years went by and rock just died
Susie went and left us for some foreign guy.
Long nights cryin' by the record machine
dreamin' of my Chevy and my old blue jeans.
But they'll never kill the thrills we've got
burning up to the crocodile rock
learning fast as the weeks went past
We really thought the crocodile rock would last, Well
(to chorus)

Daniel

Registration 2
Rhythm: Latin or Rock

Words and Music by Elton John
and Bernie Taupin

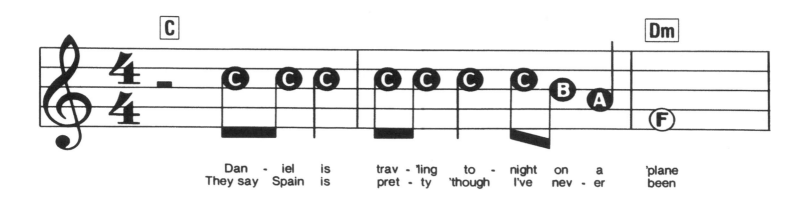

Dan - iel is trav - 'ling to - night on a 'plane
They say Spain is pret - ty 'though I've nev - er been

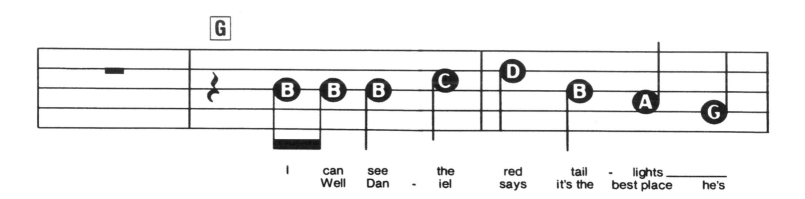

I can see the red tail - lights _____
Well Dan - iel says it's the best place he's

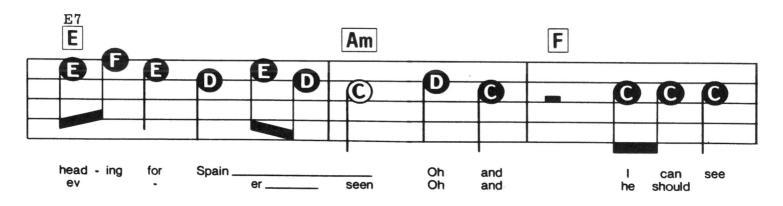

head - ing for Spain _____
ev - er _____ seen

Oh and
Oh and

I can see
he should

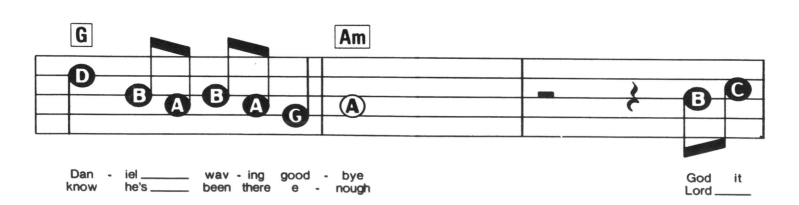

Dan - iel _____ wav - ing good - bye
know he's _____ been there e - nough

God it
Lord _____

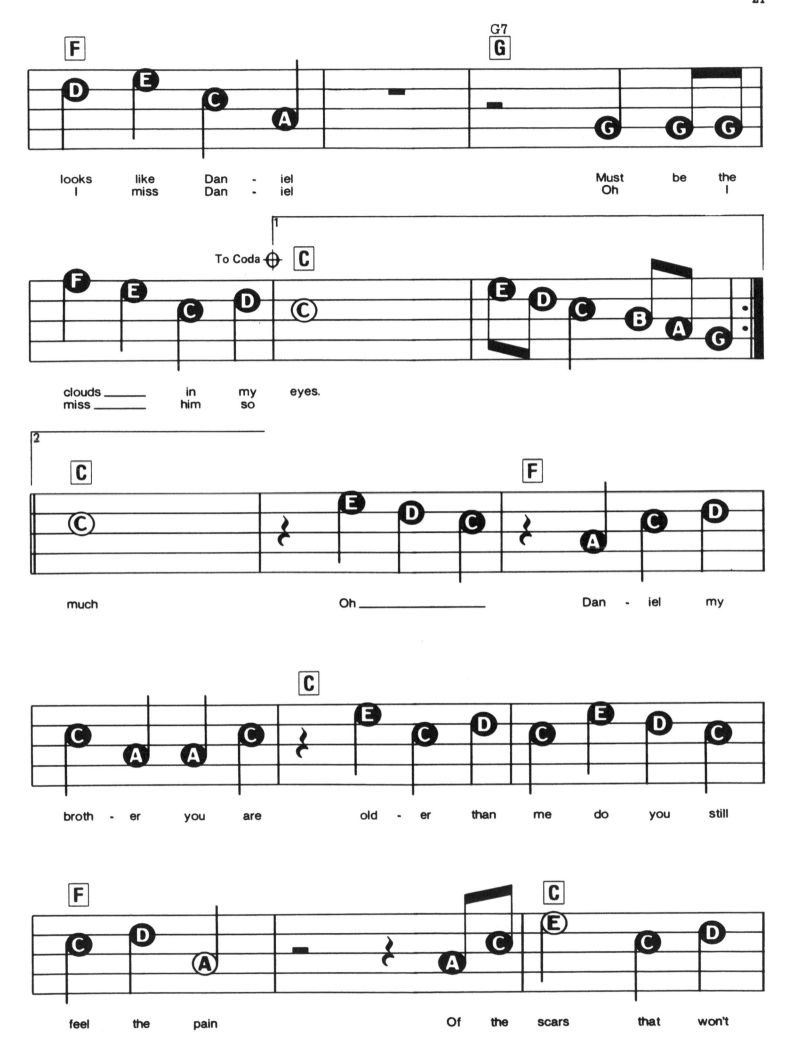

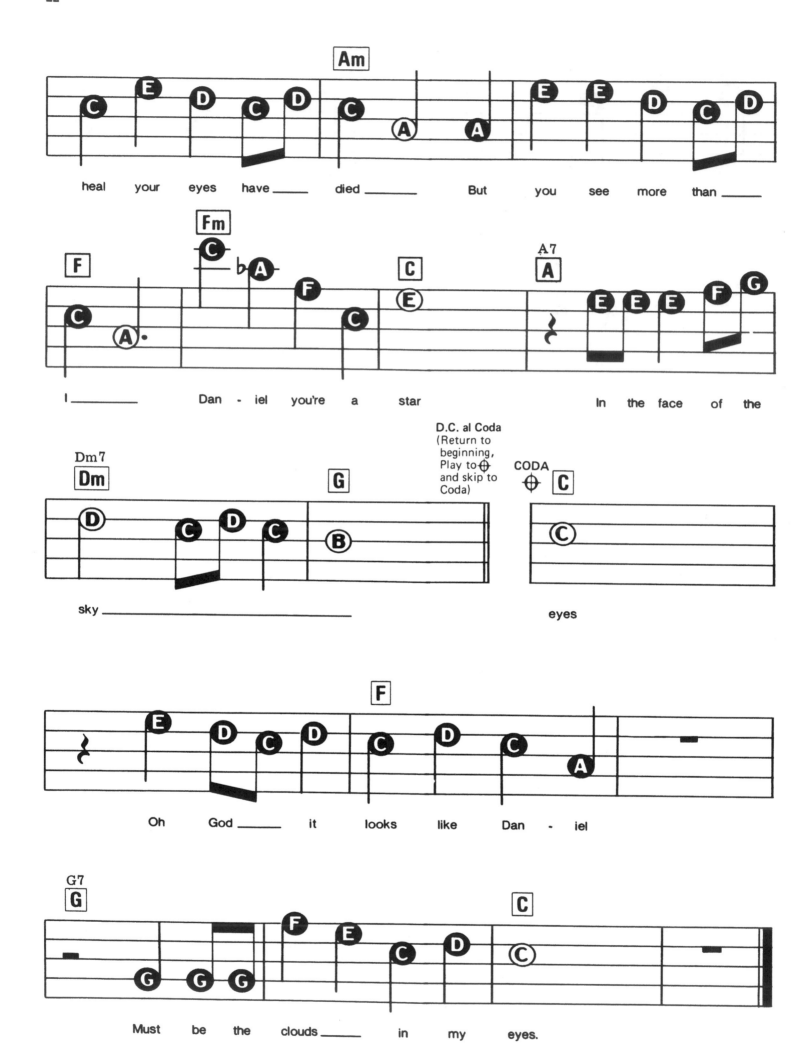

Don't Go Breaking My Heart

Registration 1
Rhythm: Swing or Pops

Words and Music by Carte Blanche
and Ann Orson

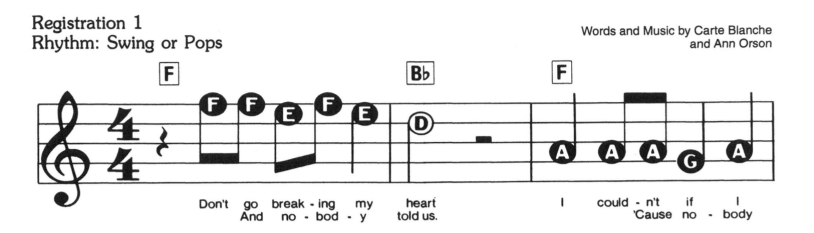

Don't go break-ing my heart
And no-bod-y told us.

I could-n't if I
'Cause no-body

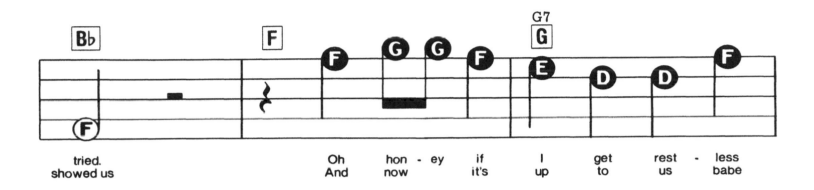

tried.
showed us

Oh hon-ey if I get rest-less
And now it's up to us babe

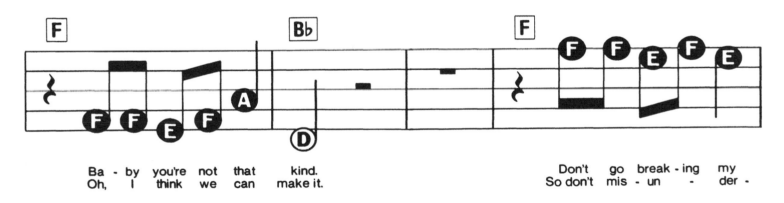

Ba-by you're not that kind.
Oh, I think we can make it.

Don't go break-ing my
So don't mis-un-der-

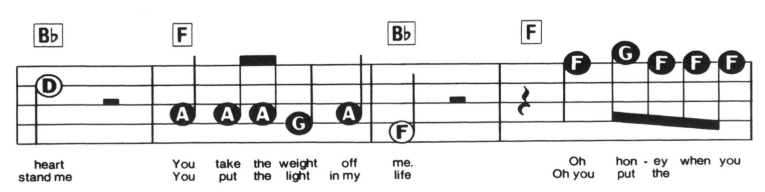

heart
stand me

You take the weight off me.
You put the light in my life

Oh hon-ey when you
Oh you put the

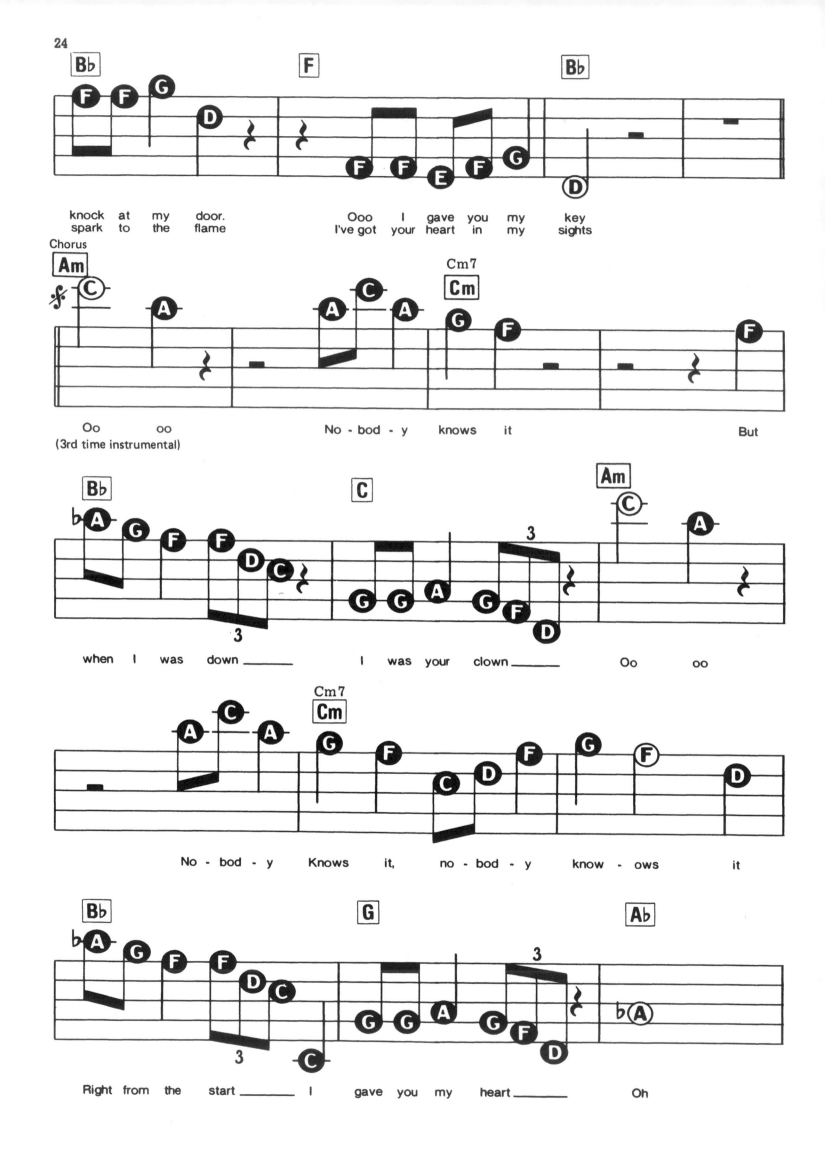

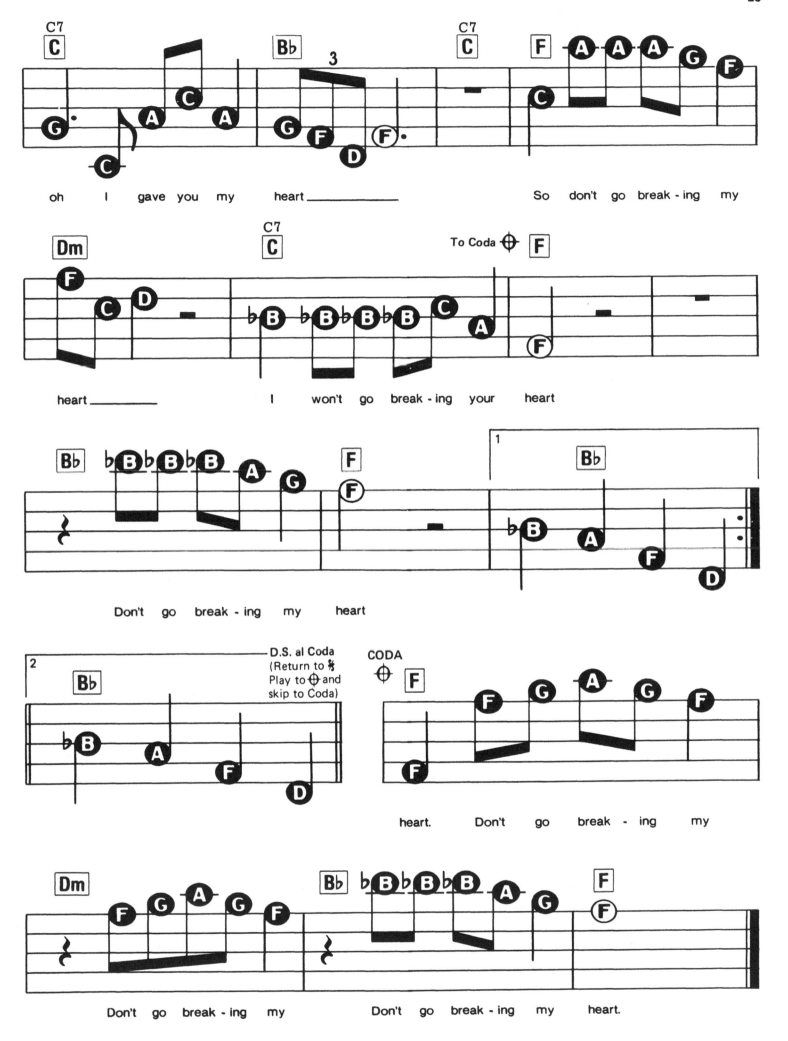

Don't Let the Sun Go Down on Me

Registration 4
Rhythm: Rock

Words and Music by Elton John
and Bernie Taupin

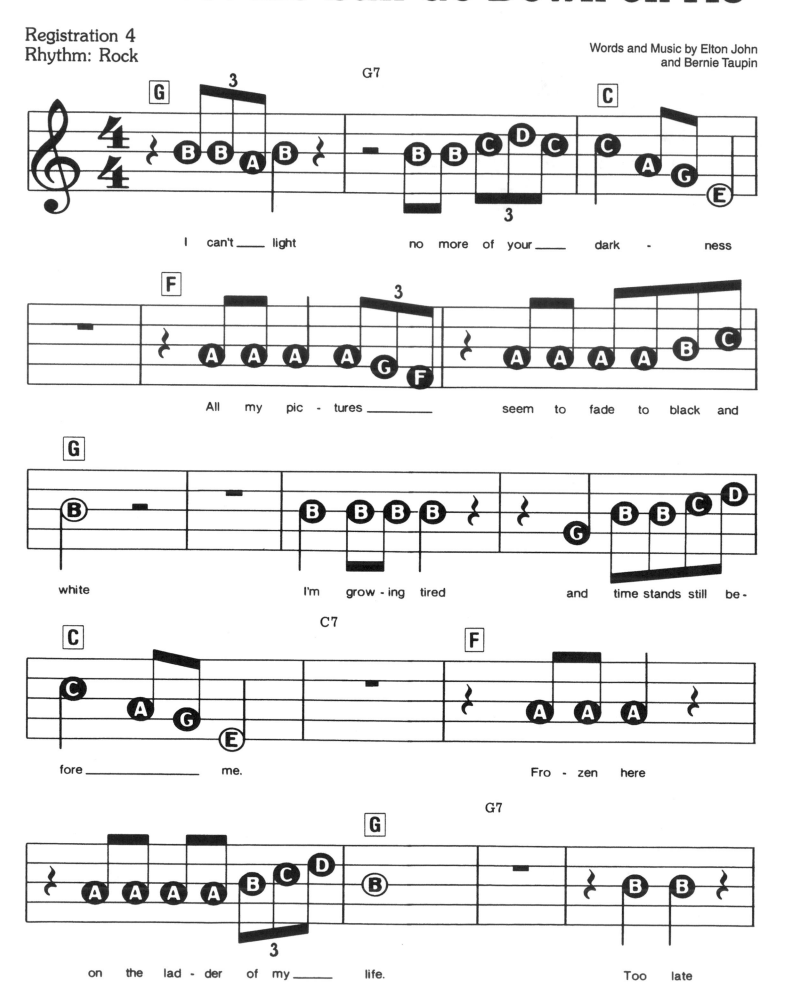

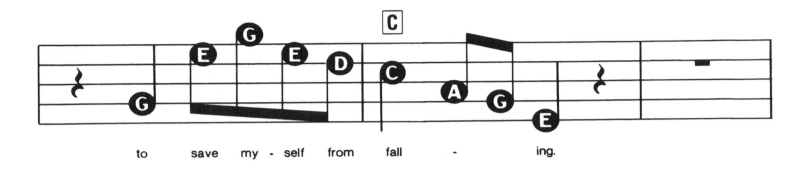

to save my - self from fall - ing.

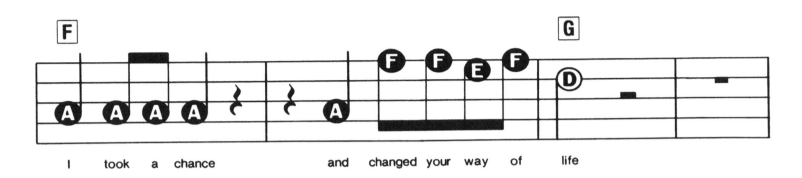

I took a chance and changed your way of life

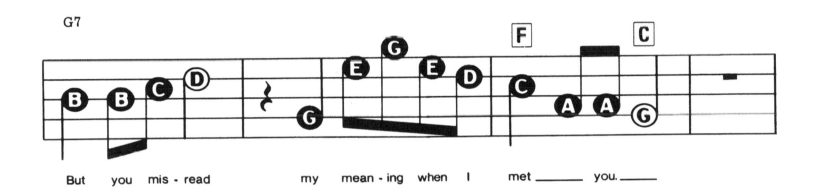

But you mis - read my mean - ing when I met ____ you. ____

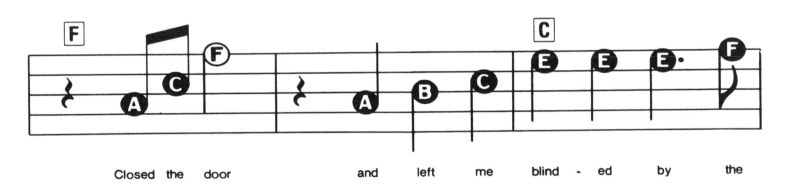

Closed the door and left me blind - ed by the

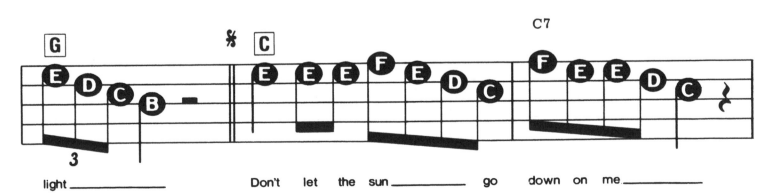

light _____ Don't let the sun ____ go down on me _____

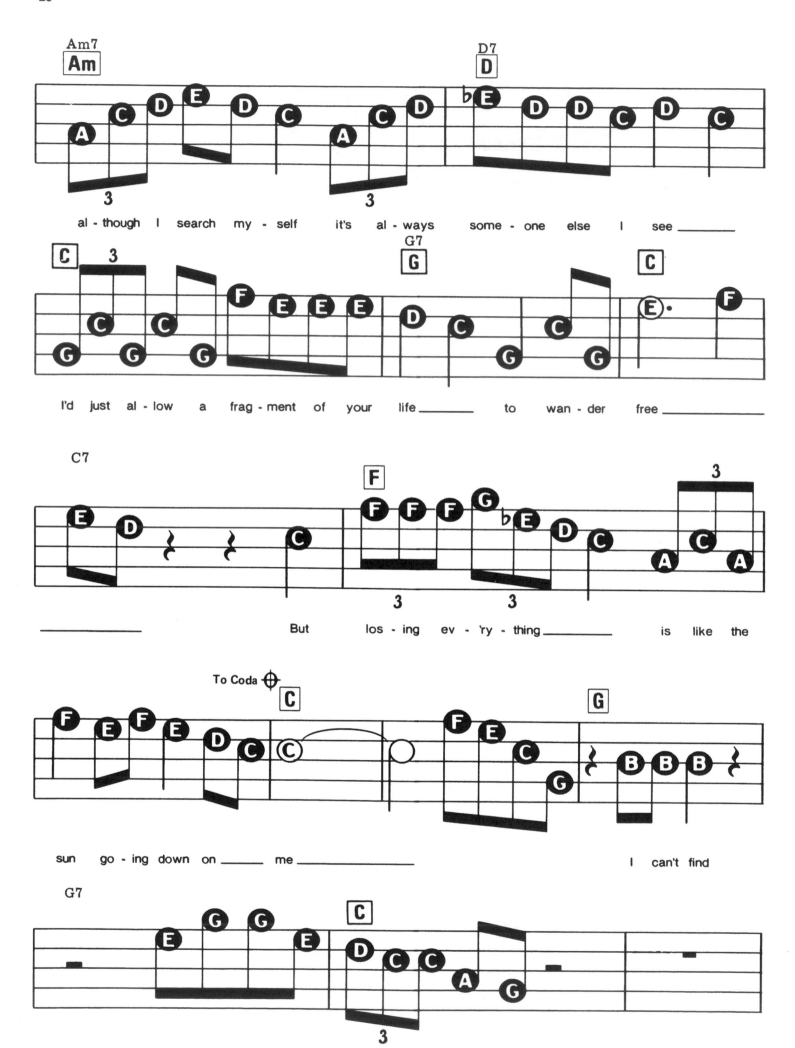

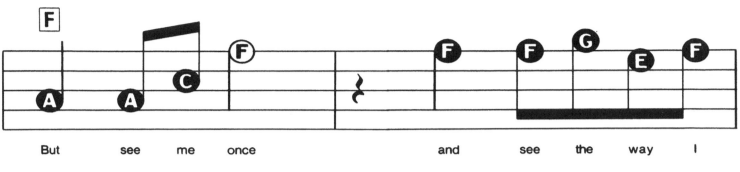

But see me once and see the way I

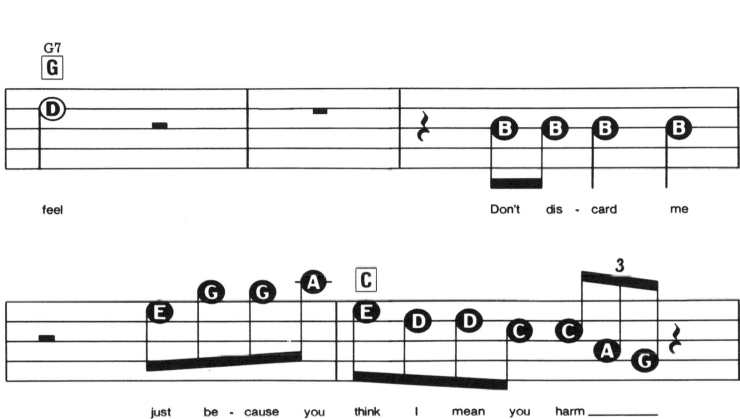

feel Don't dis - card me

just be - cause you think I mean you harm _____

But these cuts I have _____ oh they need

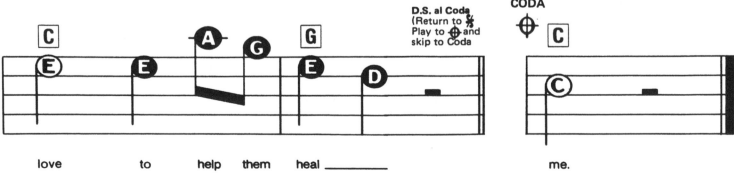

D.S. al Coda
(Return to 𝄋
Play to ⊕ and
skip to Coda

CODA ⊕

love to help them heal _____ me.

Goodbye Yellow Brick Road

Registration 5
Rhythm: Slow Rock

Words and Music by Elton John
and Bernie Taupin

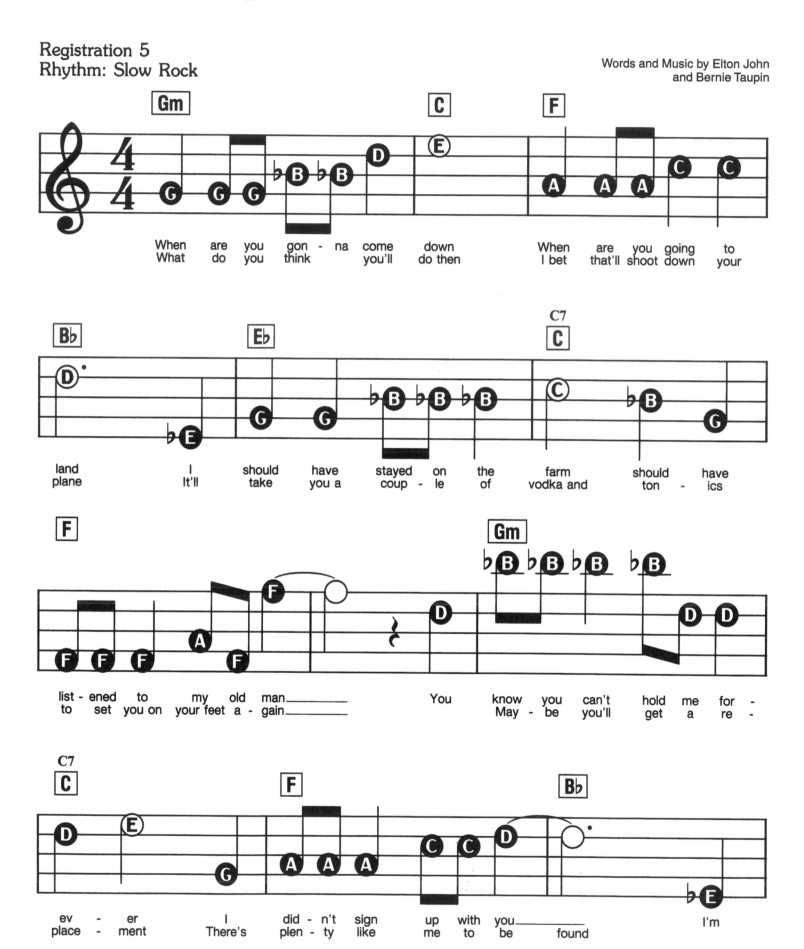

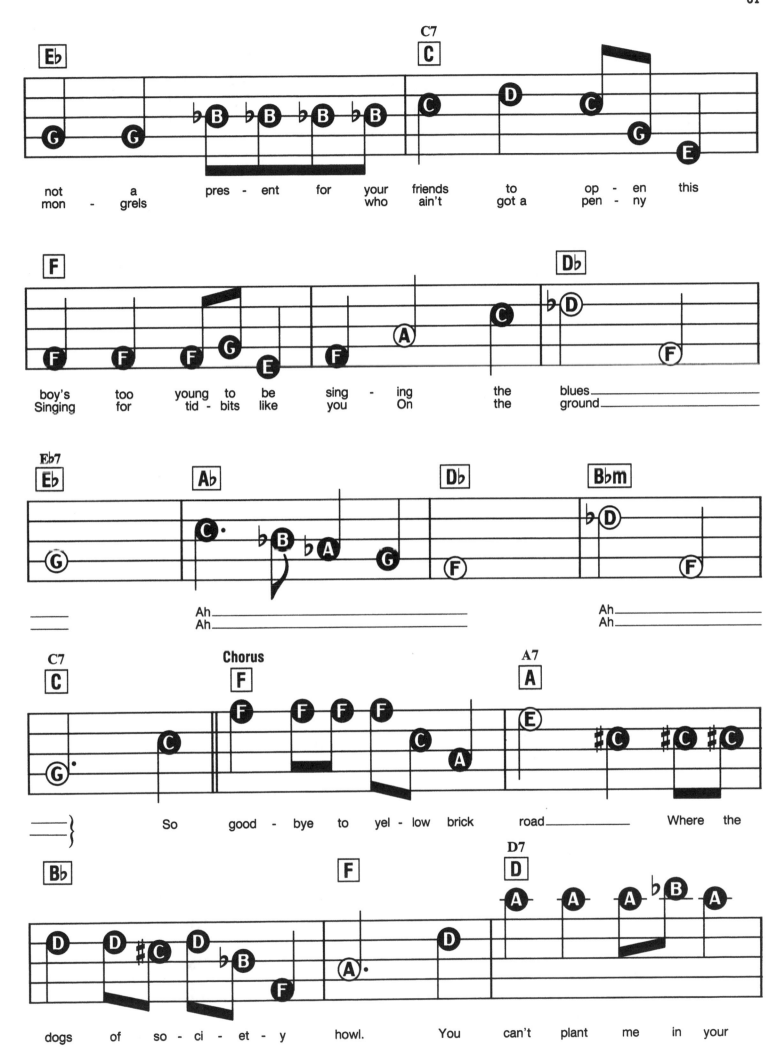

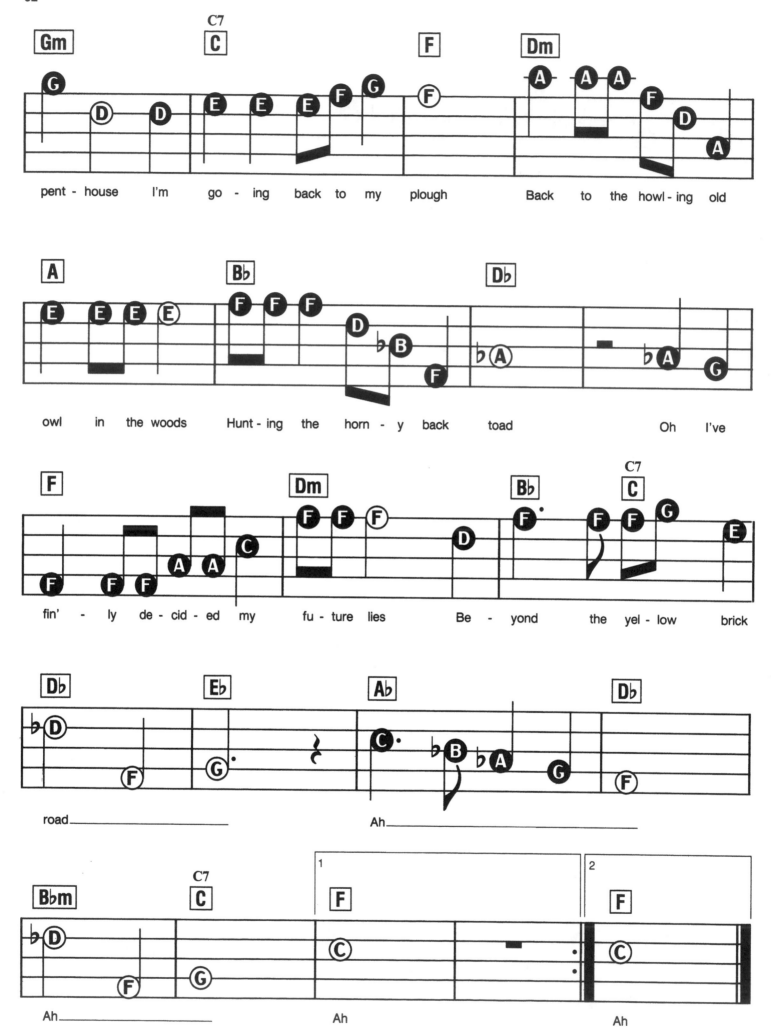

Levon

Registration 1
Rhythm: Swing or Pops

Words and Music by Elton John
and Bernie Taupin

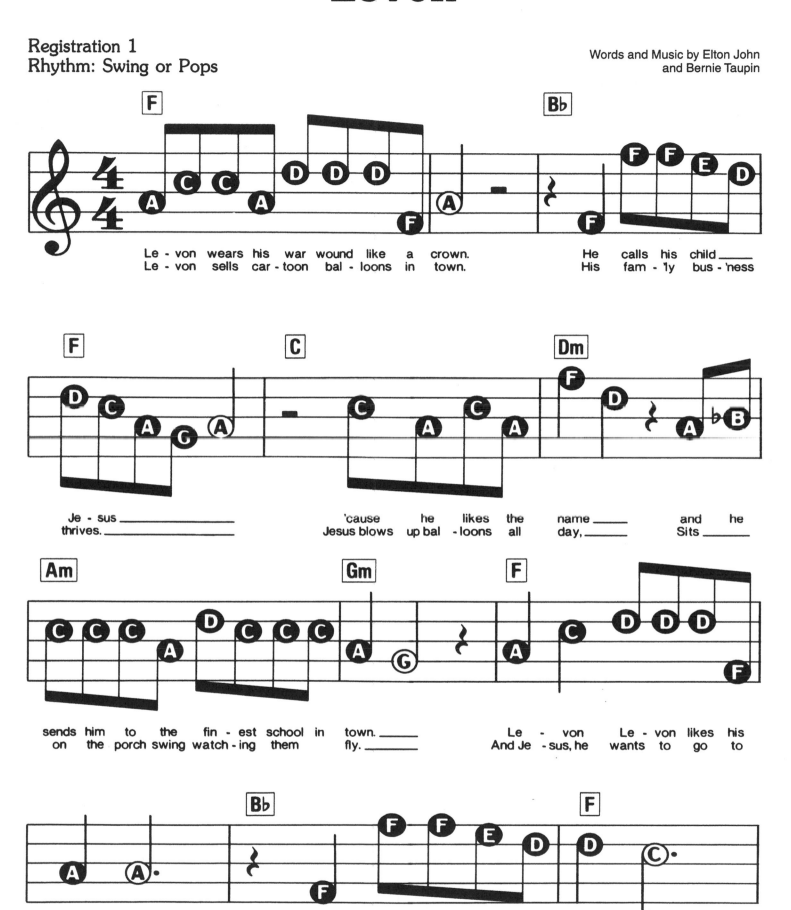

Le - von wears his war wound like a crown. He calls his child
Le - von sells car - toon bal - loons in town. His fam - 'ly bus - 'ness

Je - sus thrives. 'cause he likes the name and he
Jesus blows up bal - loons all day, Sits

sends him to the fin - est school in town. Le - von Le - von likes his
on the porch swing watch - ing them fly. And Je - sus, he wants to go to

mon - ey He makes a lot they say
Ven - us. Leave Le - von far be - hind.

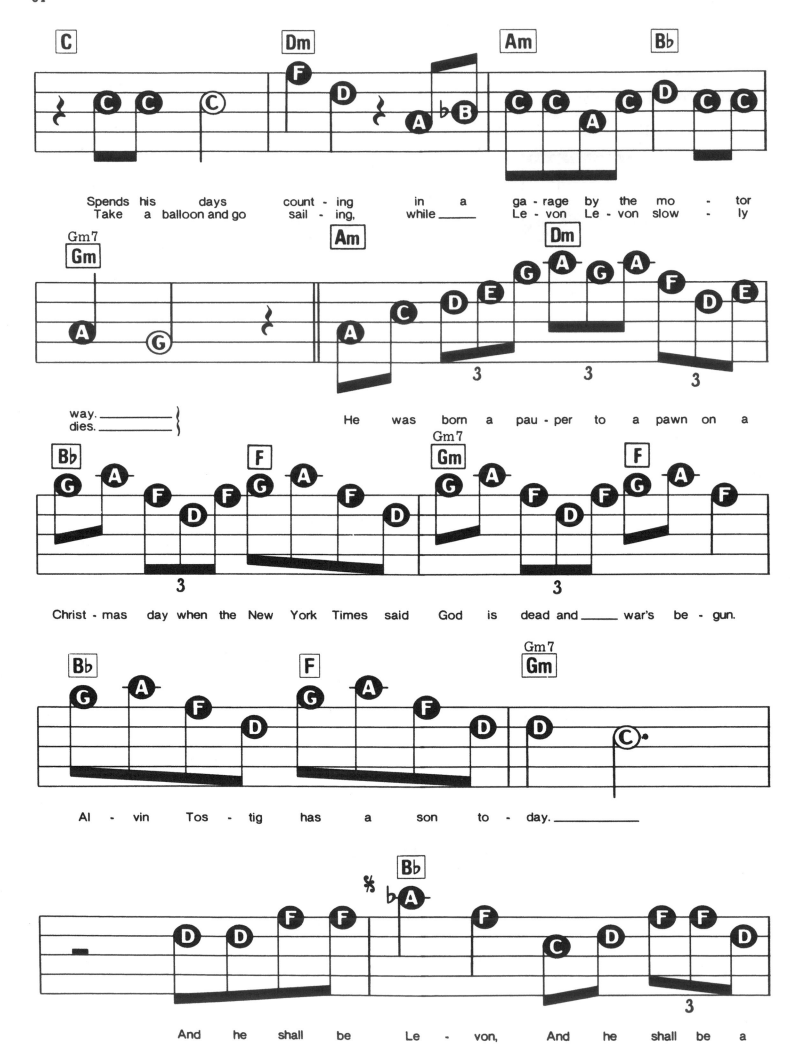

Spends his days count - ing in a ga - rage by the mo - tor
Take a balloon and go sail - ing, while _____ Le - von Le - von slow - ly

way. _____
dies. _____

He was born a pau - per to a pawn on a

Christ - mas day when the New York Times said God is dead and _____ war's be - gun.

Al - vin Tos - tig has a son to - day. _____

And he shall be Le - von, And he shall be a

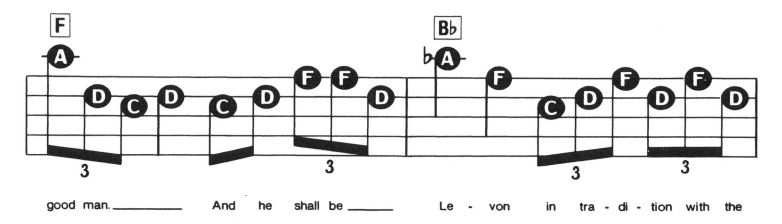

good man._____ And he shall be _____ Le - von in tra - di - tion with the

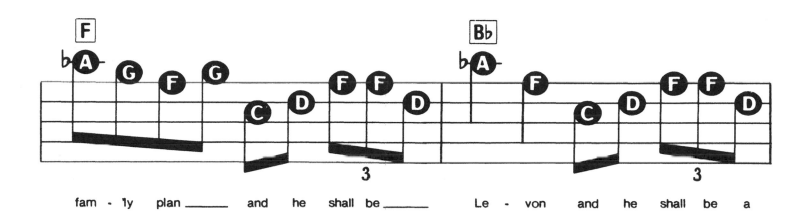

fam - 'ly plan _____ and he shall be _____ Le - von and he shall be a

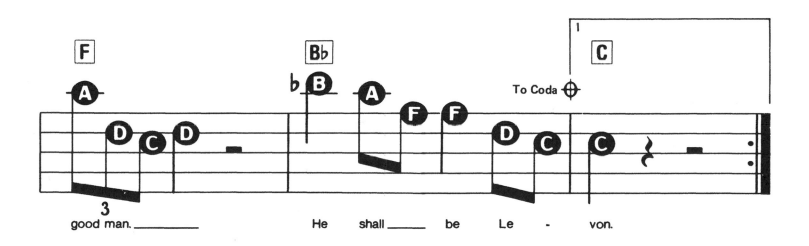

good man._____ He shall _____ be Le - von.

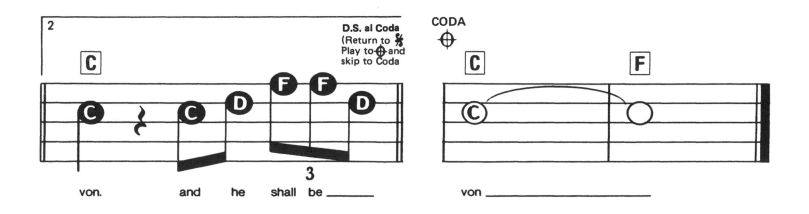

von. and he shall be _____ von _____

D.S. al Coda
(Return to 𝄋
Play to ⊕ and
skip to Coda

CODA
⊕

I Don't Wanna Go on with You Like That

Registration 5
Rhythm: Rock

Words and Music by Elton John
and Bernie Taupin

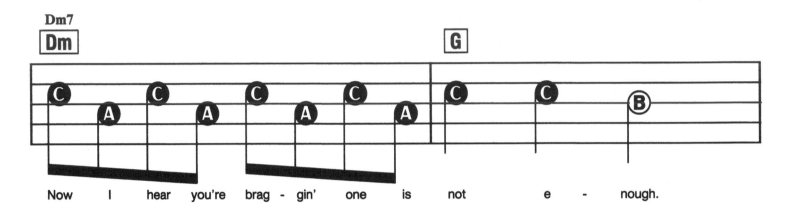

I've al-ways said that one's e-nough to love.

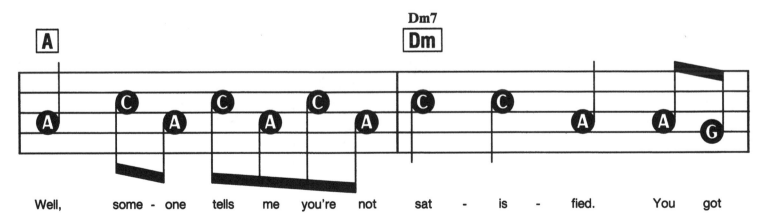

Now I hear you're brag-gin' one is not e-nough.

Well, some-one tells me you're not sat-is-fied. You got

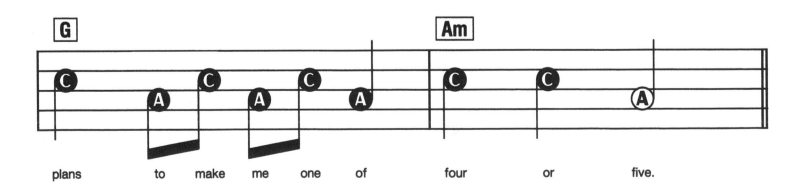

plans to make me one of four or five.

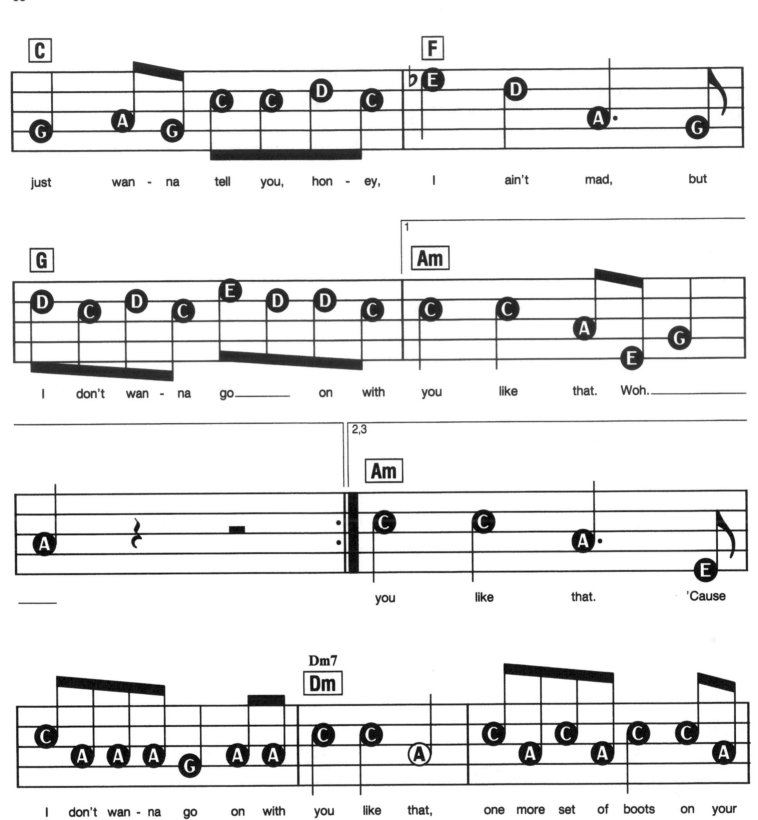

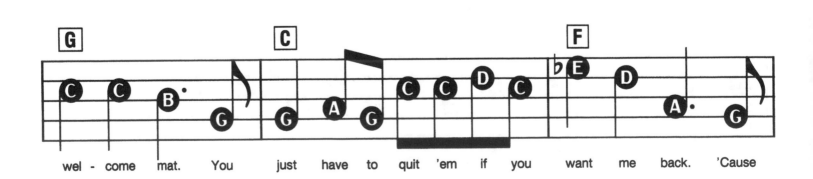

39

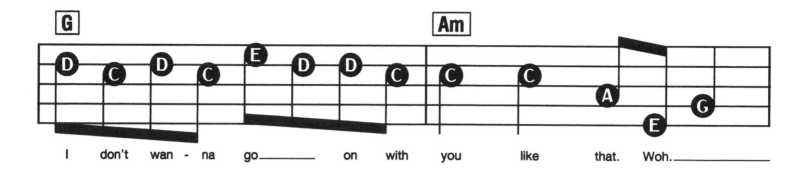

I don't wan - na go_____ on with you like that. Woh._____

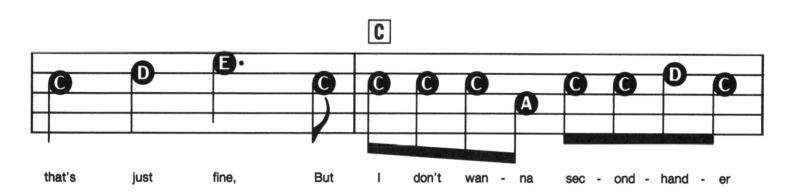

_____ Oh if you wan - na spread it a - round, sis - ter

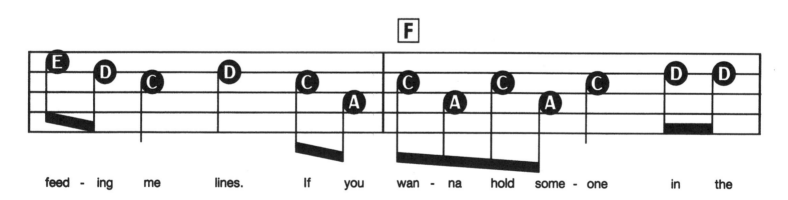

that's just fine, But I don't wan - na sec - ond - hand - er

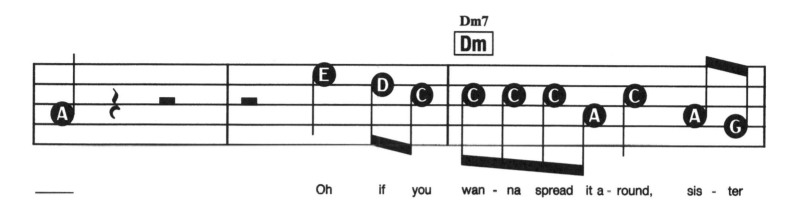

feed - ing me lines. If you wan - na hold some - one in the

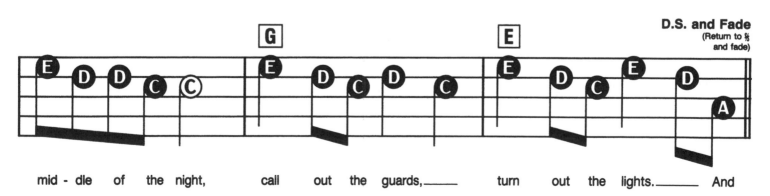

mid - dle of the night, call out the guards,_____ turn out the lights._____ And

Philadelphia Freedom

Registration 7
Rhythm: Rock or 8 Beat

Words and Music by Elton John
and Bernie Taupin

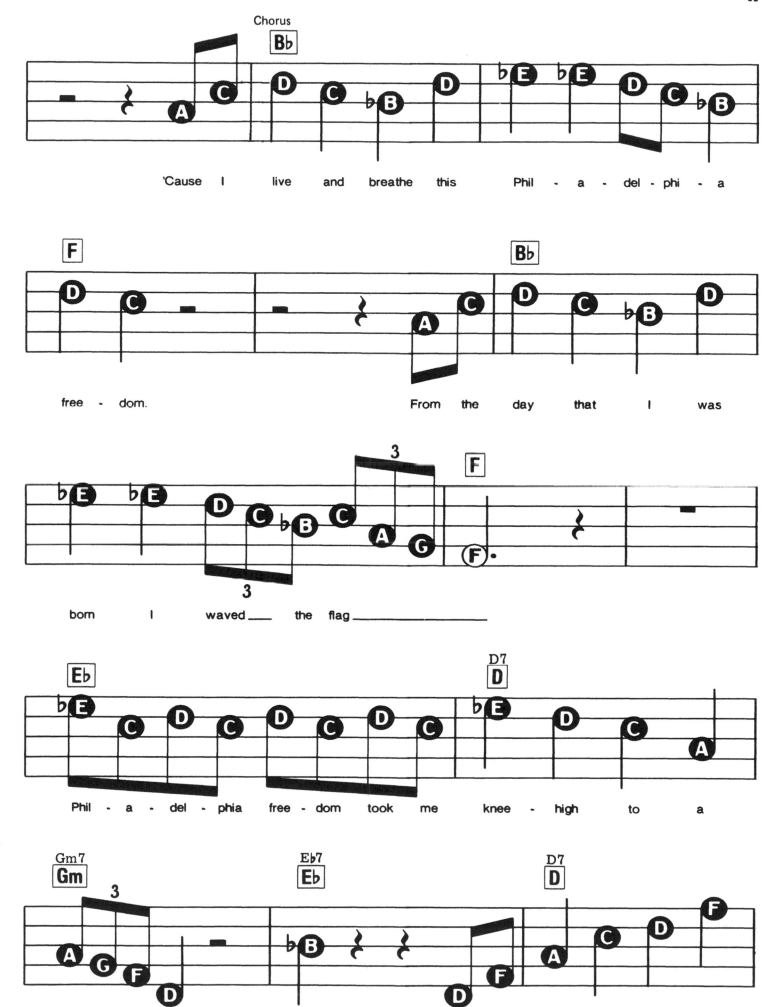

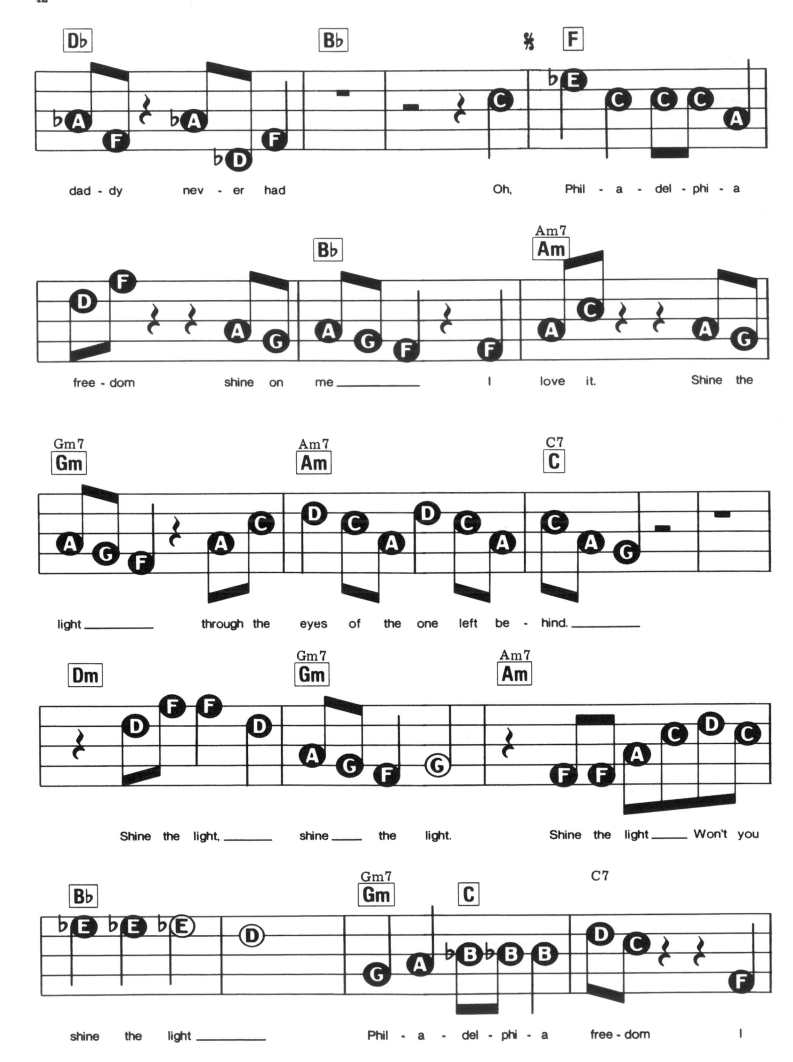

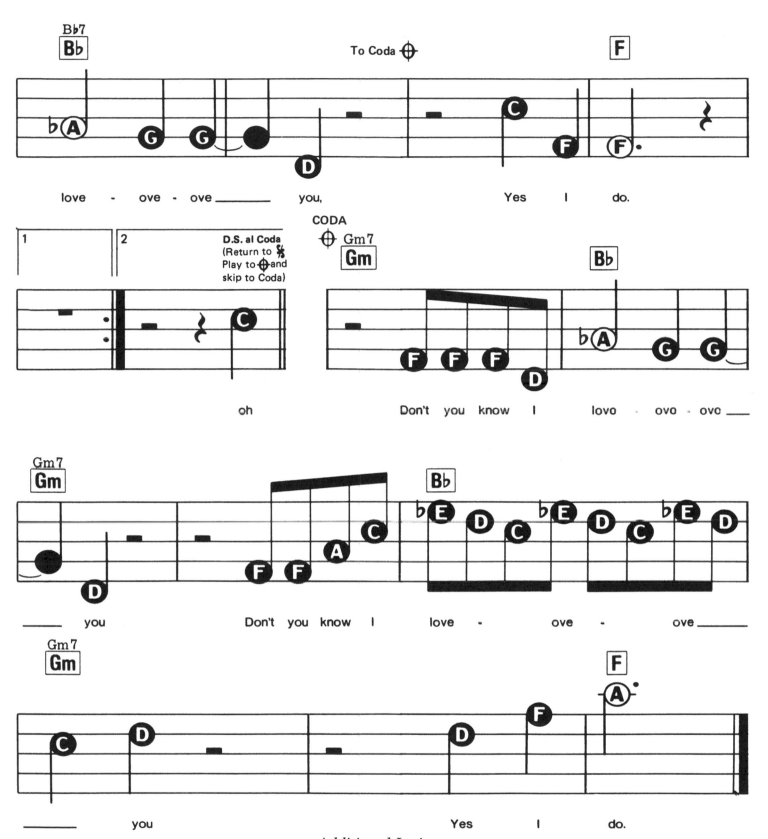

Additional Lyrics

2. If you choose to, you can live your life alone
Some people choose the city
Some others choose the good old family home
I like living easy without family ties
'Til the whippoorwill of freedom zapped me
Right between the eyes
(to Chorus)

Rocket Man
(I Think It's Gonna Be a Long Long Time)

Registration 5
Rhythm: Pops

Words and Music by Elton John
and Bernie Taupin

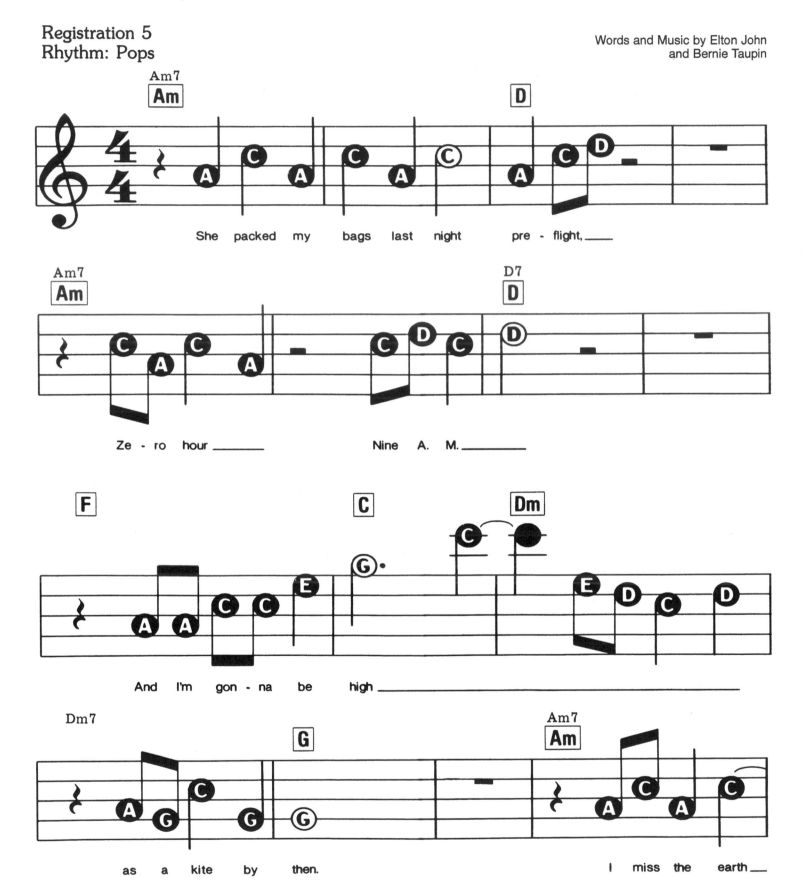

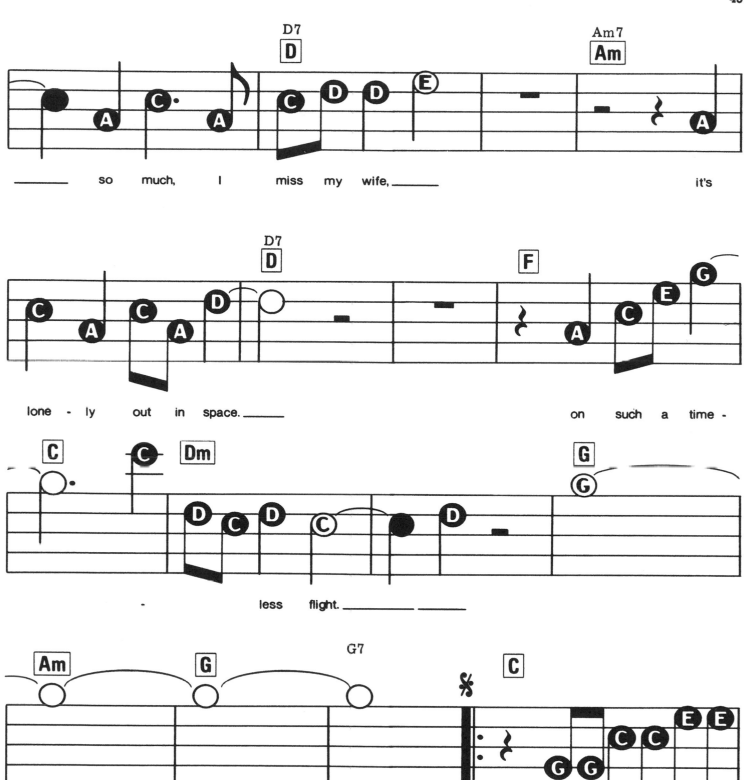

so much, I miss my wife, _____ it's

lone - ly out in space. _____ on such a time -

- less flight. _____ _____

And I think it's gon - na

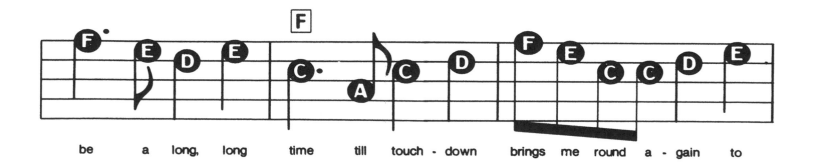

be a long, long time till touch - down brings me round a - gain to

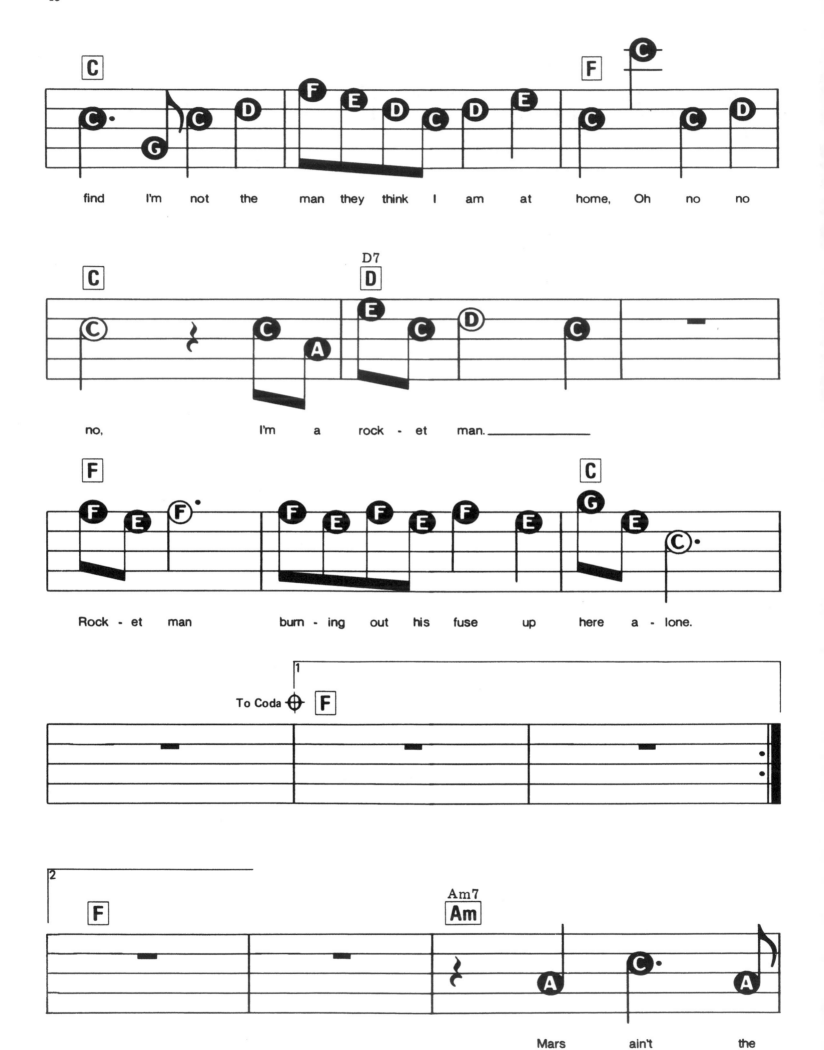

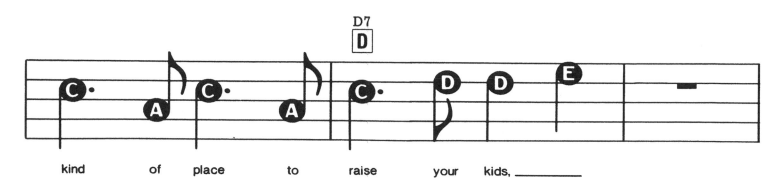

kind   of   place   to   raise   your   kids, _____

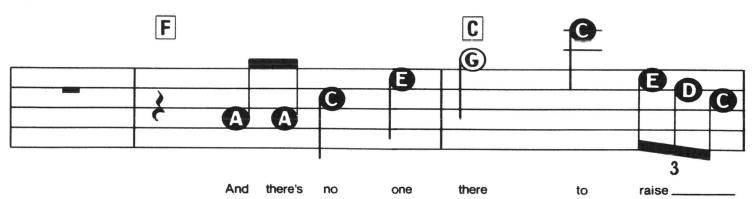

In   fact   it's   cold   as   hell. _____

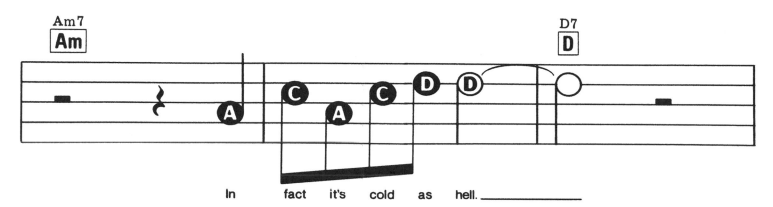

And   there's   no   one   there   to   raise _____

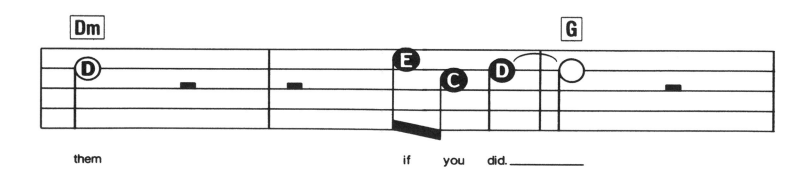

them   if   you   did. _____

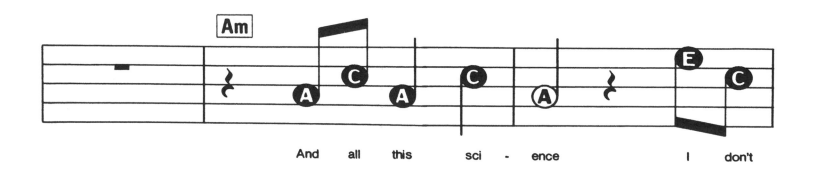

And   all   this   sci - ence   I   don't

48

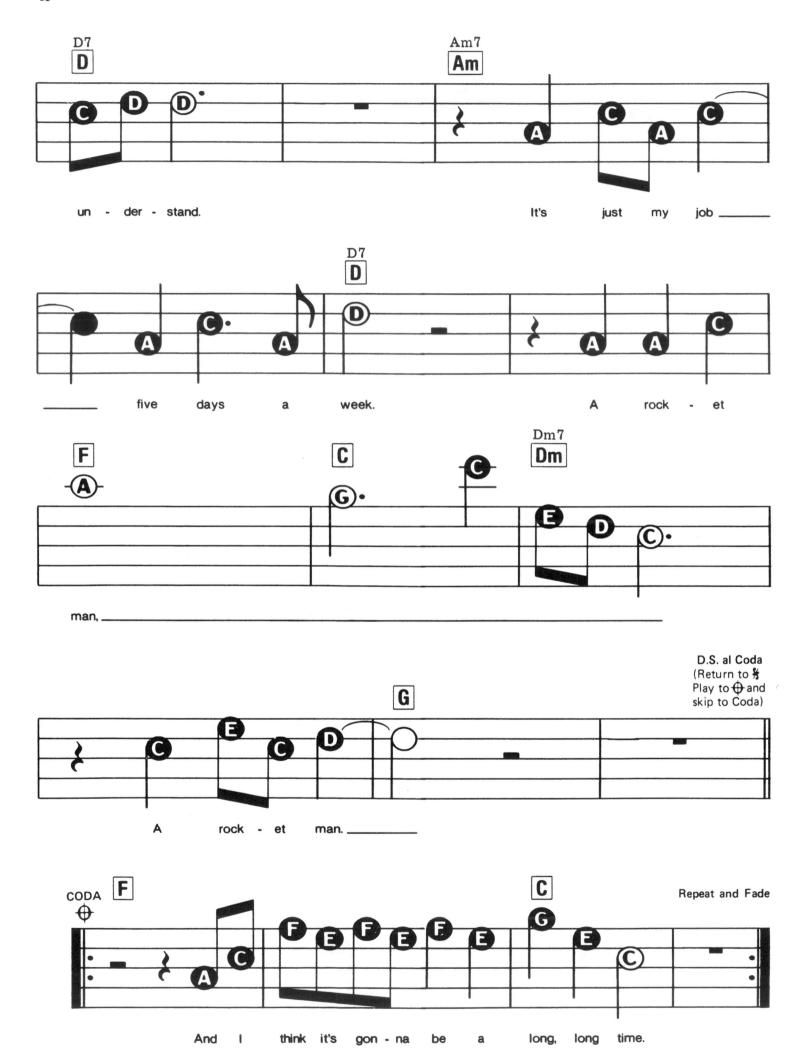

Someone Saved My Life Tonight

Registration 7
Rhythm: 8 Beat or Pops

Words and Music by Elton John
and Bernie Taupin

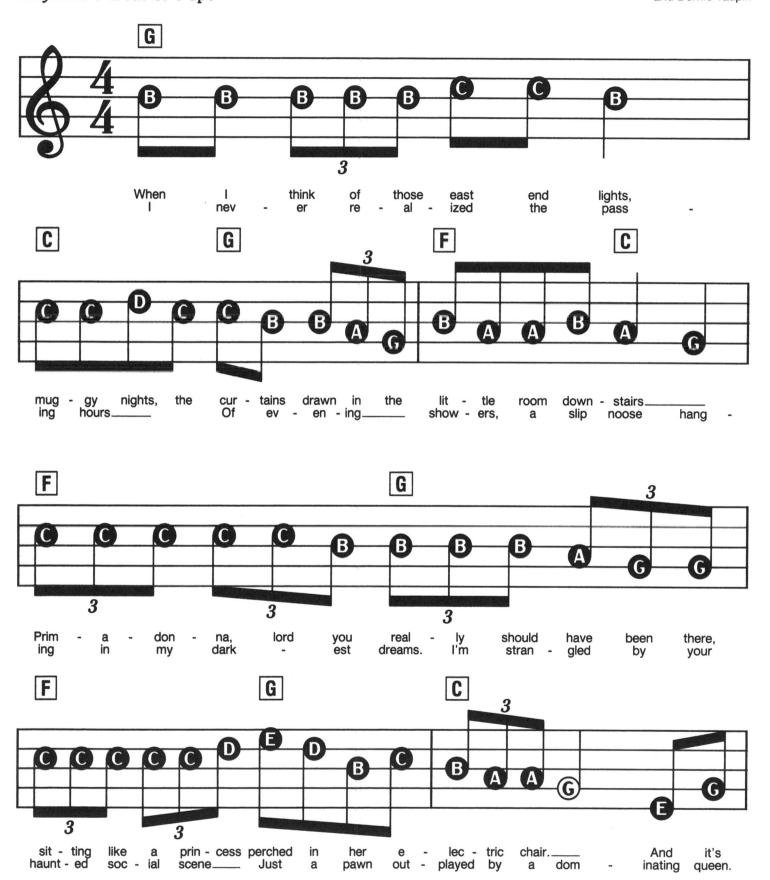

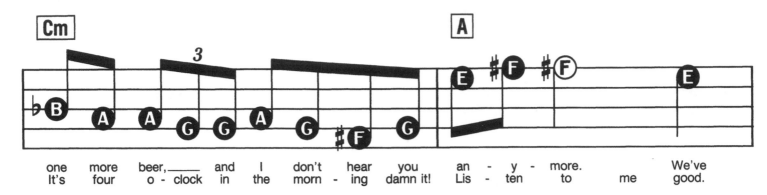

one more beer,___ and I don't hear you an - y - more. We've
It's four o - clock in the morn - ing damn it! Lis - ten to me good.

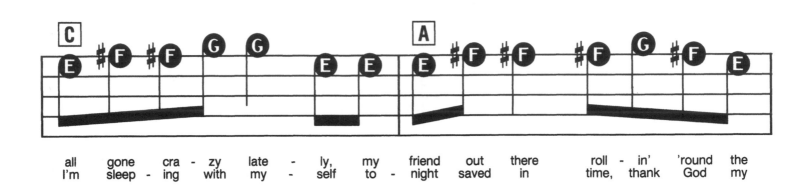

all gone cra - zy late - ly, my friend out there roll - in' 'round the
I'm sleep - ing with my - self to - night saved in time, thank God my

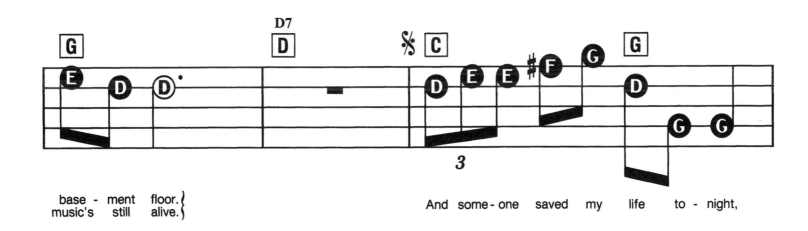

base - ment floor.⎱
music's still alive.⎰

And some - one saved my life to - night,

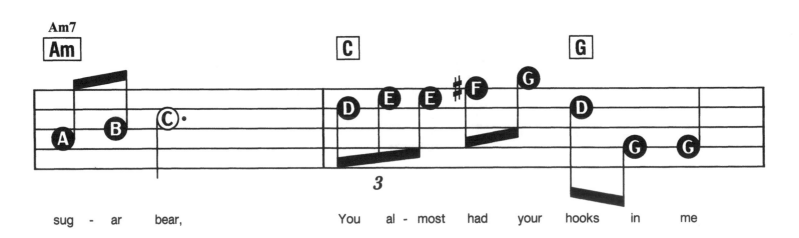

sug - ar bear,

You al - most had your hooks in me

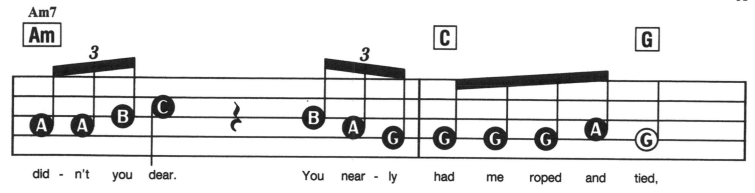

did - n't you dear.   You near - ly had me roped and tied,

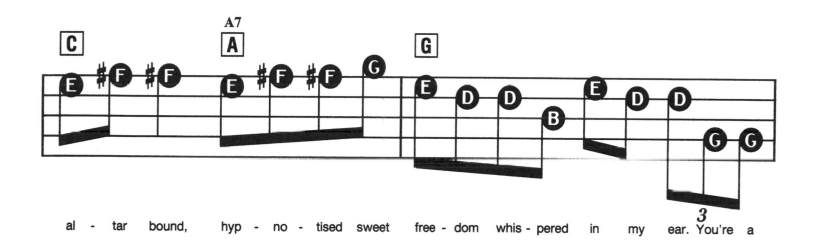

al - tar bound, hyp - no - tised sweet free - dom whis - pered in my ear. You're a

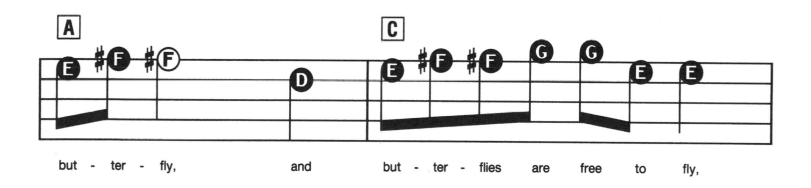

but - ter - fly,   and   but - ter - flies are free to fly,

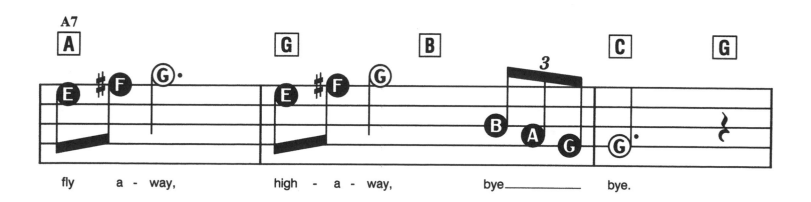

fly a - way,   high - a - way,   bye_____ bye.

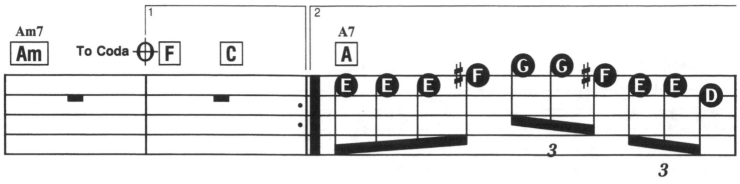

And I would have walked head on in-to the

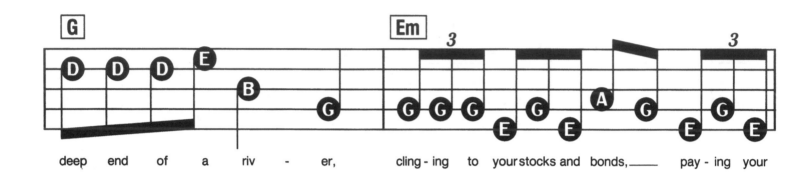

deep end of a riv - er, cling - ing to your stocks and bonds, _____ pay - ing your

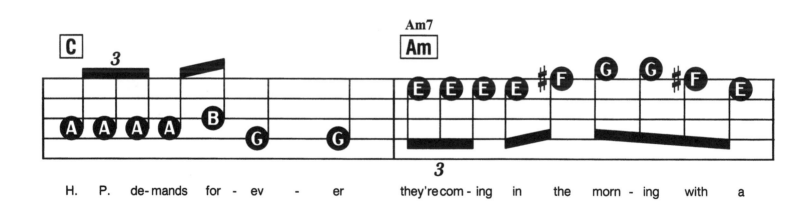

H. P. de-mands for - ev - er they're com - ing in the morn - ing with a

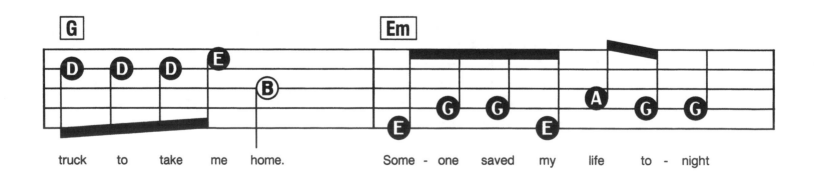

truck to take me home. Some - one saved my life to - night

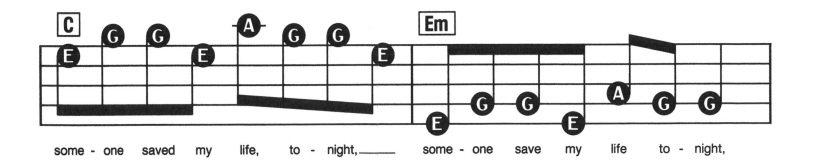

some - one saved my life, to - night,_____ some - one save my life to - night,

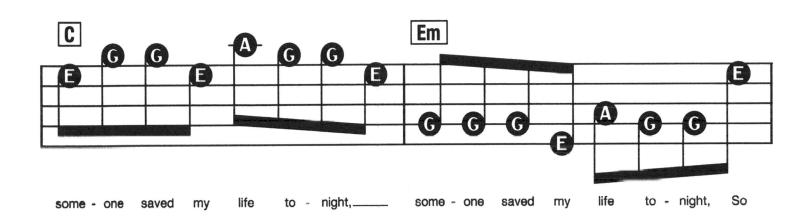

some - one saved my life to - night,_____ some - one saved my life to - night, So

D.S. al Coda
(Return to %
Play to ⊕ and
skip to Coda)

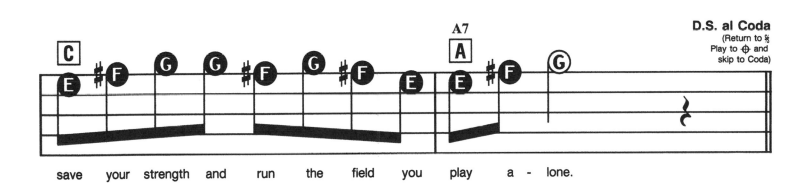

save your strength and run the field you play a - lone.

Repeat and Fade

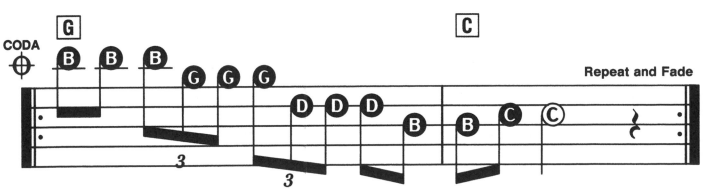

Some - one saved, some - one saved, some - one saved my life to - night.

Sorry Seems to Be the Hardest Word

Registration 8
Rhythm: 8 Beat or Pops

Words and Music by Elton John
and Bernie Taupin

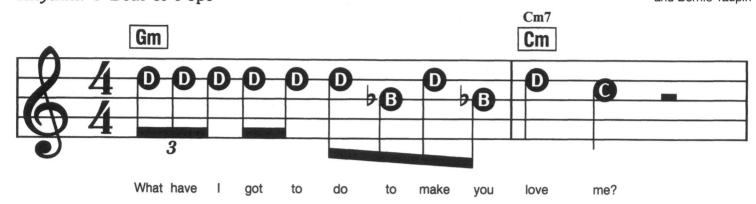

What have I got to do to make you love me?

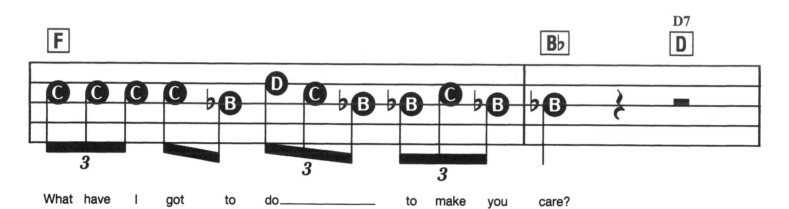

What have I got to do_____ to make you care?

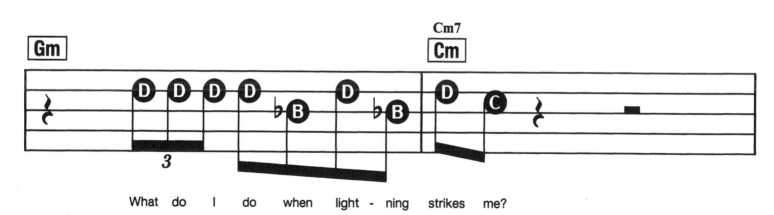

What do I do when light - ning strikes me?

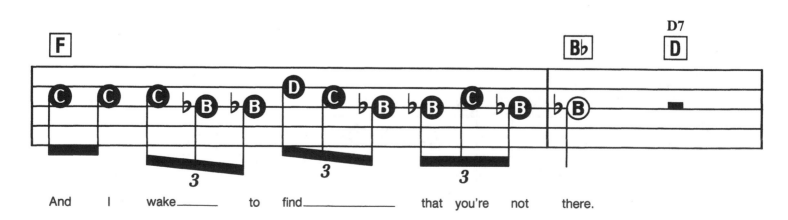

And I wake_____ to find_____ that you're not there.

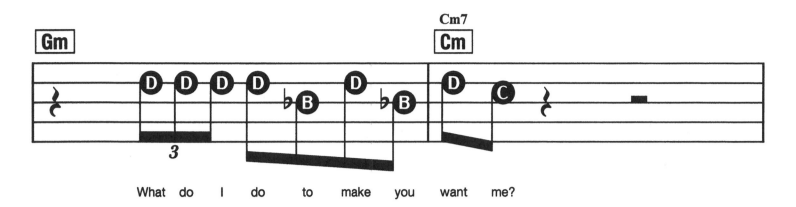

What do I do to make you want me?

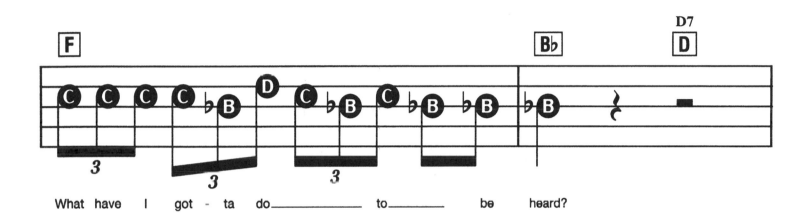

What have I got-ta do_____ to_____ be heard?

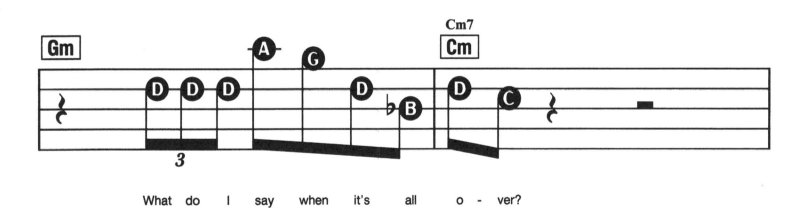

What do I say when it's all o - ver?

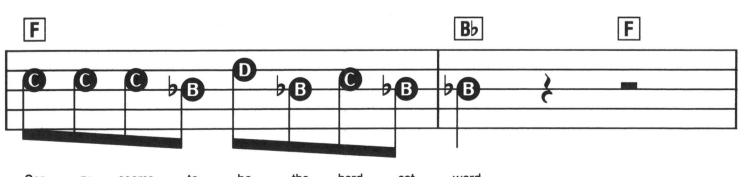

Sor - ry seems to be the hard - est word.

55

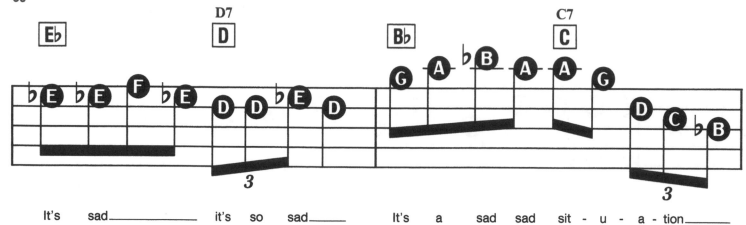

It's sad_____ it's so sad_____ It's a sad sad sit - u - a - tion_____

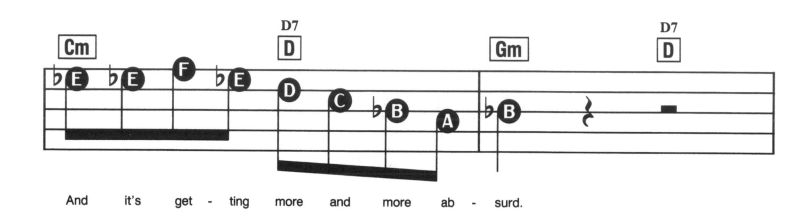

And it's get - ting more and more ab - surd.

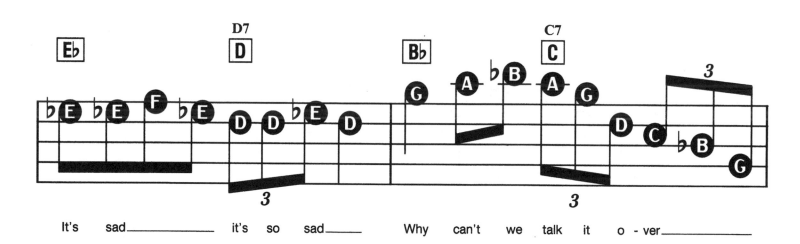

It's sad_____ it's so sad_____ Why can't we talk it o - ver_____

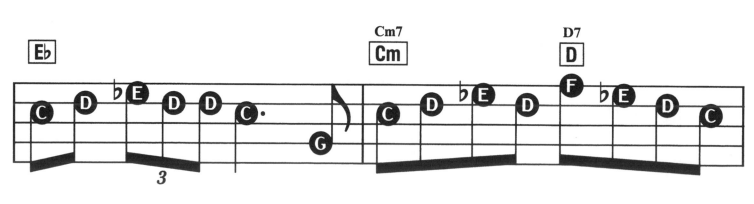

Al - ways seems to me_____ that sor - ry seems to be the hard - est

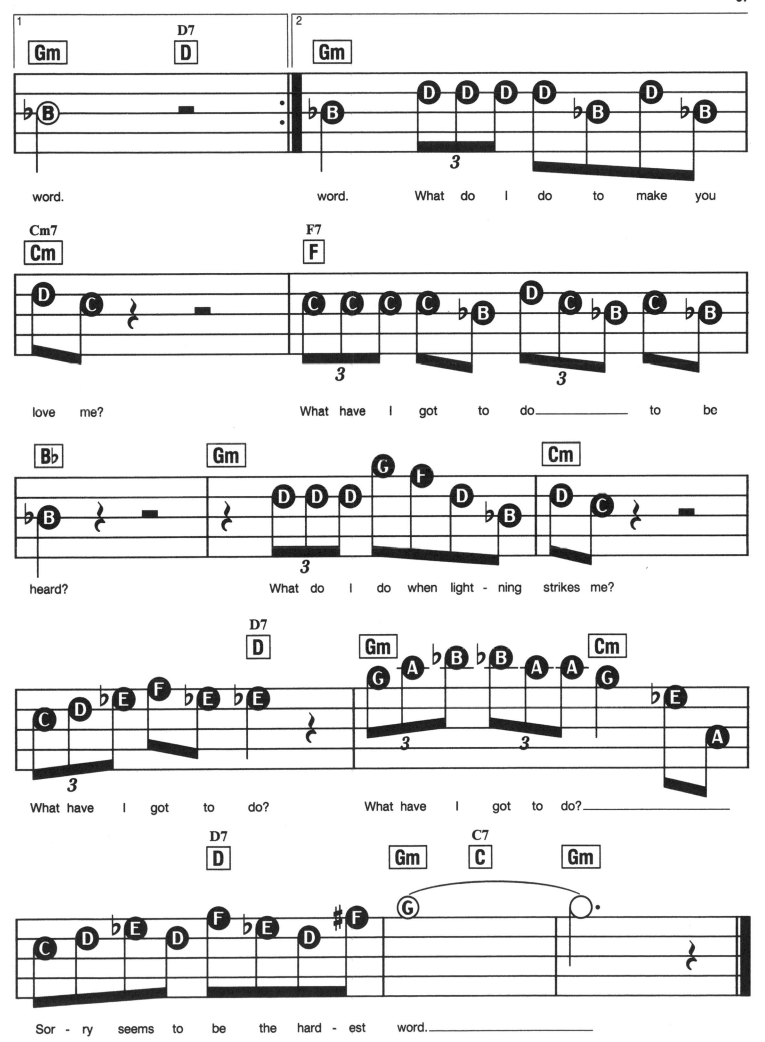

Your Song

Registration 3
Rhythm: Rock or Jazz Rock

Words and Music by Elton John
and Bernie Taupin

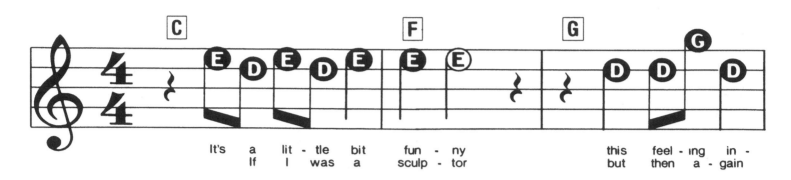

It's a lit - tle bit fun - ny this feel - ing in -
If I was a sculp - tor but then a - gain

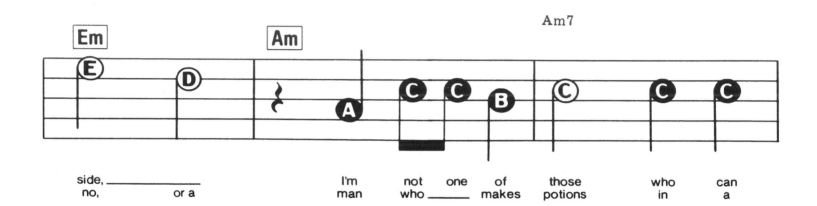

side, _____ no, or a I'm man not who ___ one of makes those potions who in can a

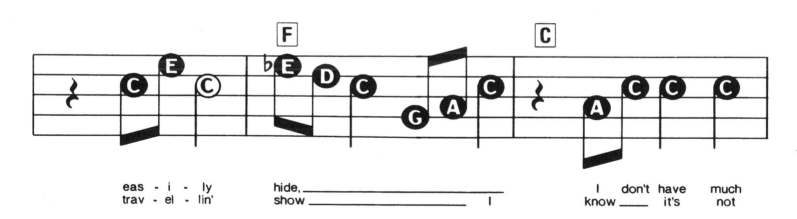

eas - i - ly hide, _____ I don't have much
trav - el - lin' show _____ I know ___ it's much not

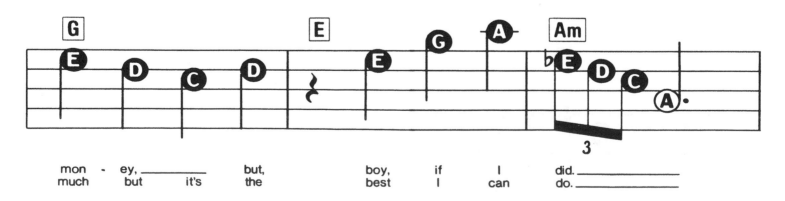

mon - ey, _____ but, boy, if I did. _____
much but it's the best I can do. _____

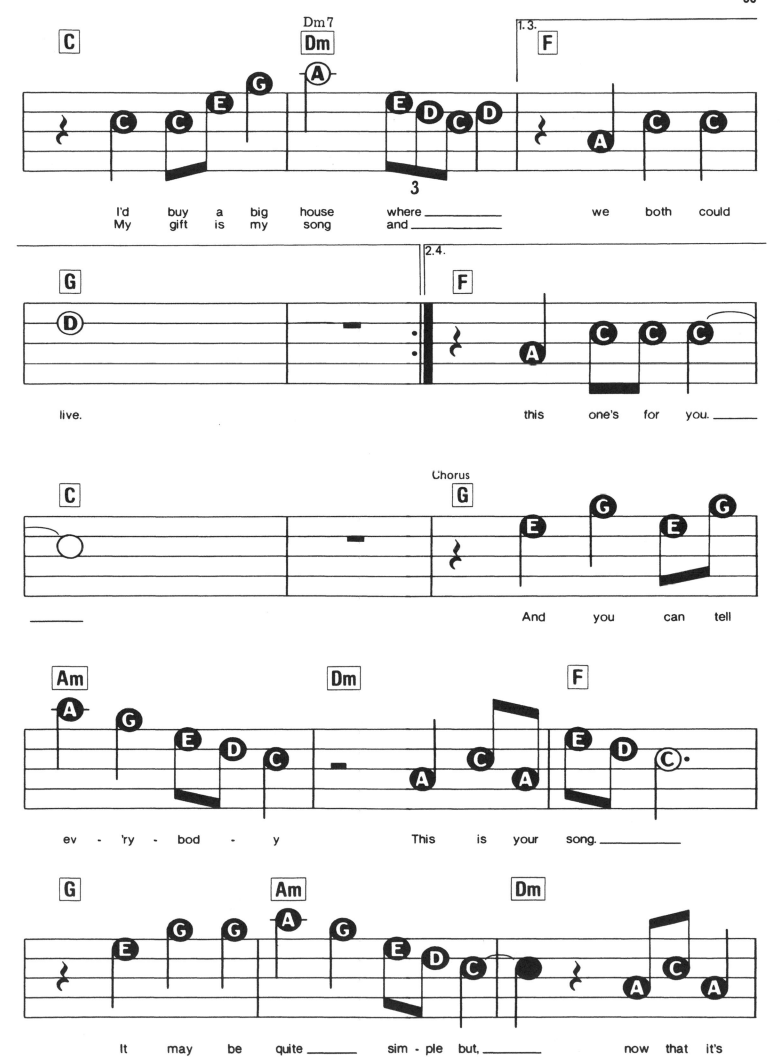

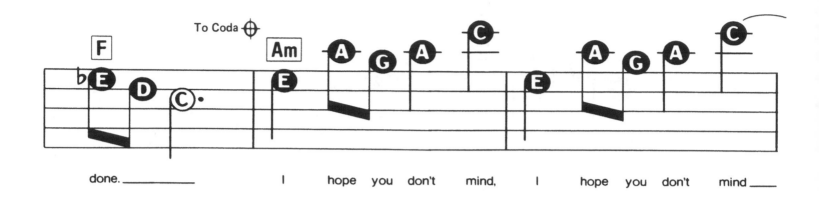

done._____ I hope you don't mind, I hope you don't mind ___

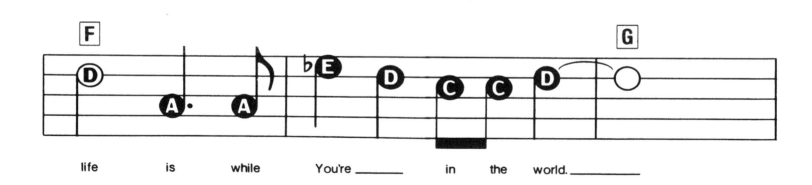

___ that I put down in ___ words. How won - der - ful

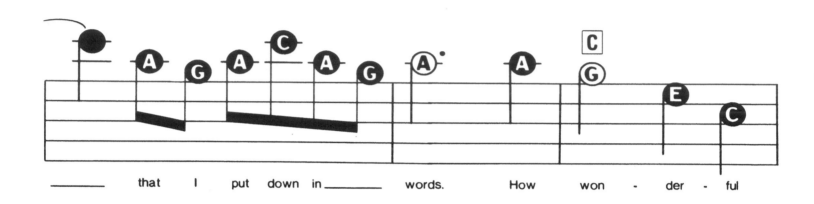

life is while You're ___ in the world. ___

D.C. al Coda
(Return to beginning, take 3rd & 4th endings, Play till ⊕ and skip to Coda)

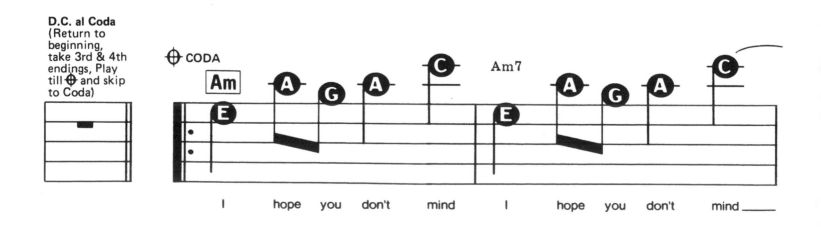

I hope you don't mind I hope you don't mind ___

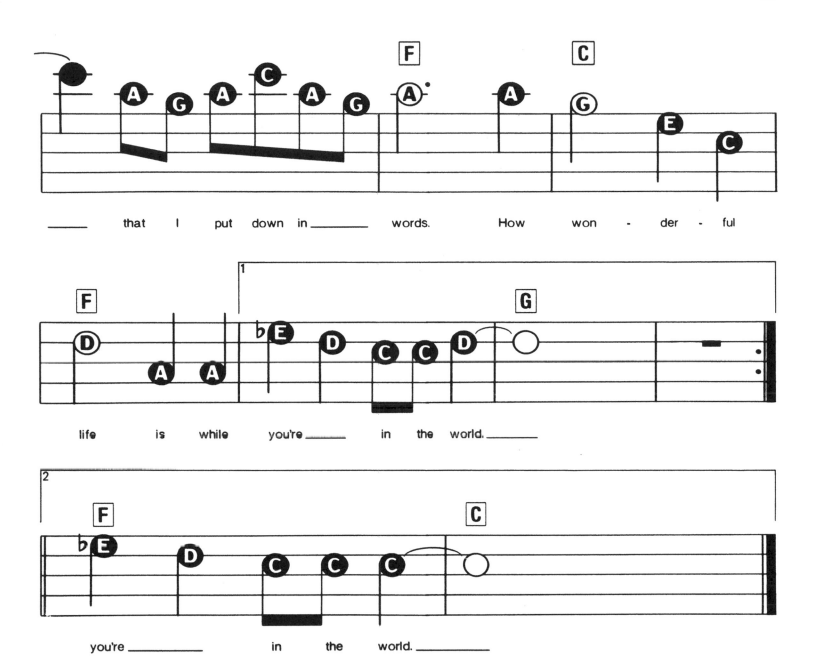

that I put down in _____ words. How won - der - ful

life is while you're _____ in the world. _____

you're _____ in the world. _____

3. I sat on the roof and kicked off the moss.
well a few of the verses, well they've got me quite cross,
But the sun's been quite kind while I wrote this song,
It's for people like you that keep it turned on.

4. So excuse me forgetting but these things I do
You see I've forgotten if they're green or they're blue,
Anyway the thing is what I really mean
Yours are the sweetest eyes I've ever seen.

Registration Guide

- Match the Registration number on the song to the corresponding numbered category below. Select and activate an instrumental sound available on your instrument.

- Choose an automatic rhythm appropriate to the mood and style of the song. (Consult your Owner's Guide for proper operation of automatic rhythm features.)

- Adjust the tempo and volume controls to comfortable settings.

Registration

1	Flute, Pan Flute, Jazz Flute
2	Clarinet, Organ
3	Violin, Strings
4	Brass, Trumpet
5	Synth Ensemble, Accordion, Brass
6	Pipe Organ, Harpsichord
7	Jazz Organ, Vibraphone, Vibes, Electric Piano, Jazz Guitar
8	Piano, Electric Piano
9	Trumpet, Trombone, Clarinet, Saxophone, Oboe
10	Violin, Cello, Strings